WAR

Disco**ﾕｰders**
Tｒiumphs

DEBRA GREEN **JOSH GREEN**

Copyright © Josh Green and Debra Green OBE

First published 2025 by Redeeming Our Communities.

www.roc.uk.com/waymaker

The right of Josh Green and Debra Green to be identified as the author of this work has been asserted by them in accordance with the Copyright, Designs and Patents Act 1988.

All rights reserved.

No part of this publication may be reproduced, stored in a retrieval system, or transmitted in any other form or by any means, electronic, mechanical, photocopying, recording or otherwise, without the prior permission of the publisher, except in the case of brief quotations embodied in critical articles or reviews.

British Library Cataloguing in Publication Data. A catalogue record for this book is available from the British Library.

ISBN: 978-1-0369-1379-3

Cover design by Josh Mellor

CONTENTS

Acknowledgements   5

Chapter 1   Show Me Your Ways (Debra/Josh)   7

PART 1:   WAY MAKER
Chapter 2   Walking Through Fire (Debra)   23
Chapter 3   The Prayer God Always Answers (Josh)   43

PART 2:   MIRACLE WORKER
Chapter 4   Battles and Breakthroughs (Josh)   67
Chapter 5   There Can be Miracles (Debra)   89

PART 3:   PROMISE KEEPER
Chapter 6   Good News Stories (Debra)   111
Chapter 7   Your Honour is at Stake (Josh)   131

PART 4:   LIGHT BRINGER
Chapter 8   Redeeming our Communities (Debra)   157
Chapter 9   Shining like Stars (Josh)   181

Chapter 10   As He is, So Are We (Debra/Josh)   203

Endorsements   211
Bios   217

ACKNOWLEDGEMENTS

Our heartfelt thanks to those who have helped us to prepare and publish this book, including Dr Mark Stibbe (BookLab), Josh Mellor (graphics), Esther Kotecha, and Frank Green. Thanks also to those who have given permission for us to use material (said or sung), and to our dear friend Steve Legg who told me to write this book! Thanks to those who have taken the time to read the manuscript and graciously endorse the book.

From Debra: thank you to my wonderful family, my husband Frank, our four grownup children and seven grandchildren who always put a smile on my face. My heartfelt thanks to the staff at Salford Royal hospital who looked after me during my illness.

From Josh: this book is dedicated with thanks to my beautiful wife and wonderful children. We have journeyed through so much over the years. There have been tears and laughter, pain and purpose, songs and suffering, highs and lows, mountains and valleys, and everything between, *but* God has been, and will always be, with us through it all. May we never stop following him with everything. May we always thank him for what he has done, believe for miracles, trust in his promises, be a light to those around us, and know he will always make a way.

CHAPTER 1
SHOW ME YOUR WAYS

President Abraham Lincoln once said, "I remember my mother's prayers and they have always followed me. They have clung to me all my life."[1] If there is one thing I, Debra, have done right in parenting my son Josh, it's that I've prayed for him. Prayer is what has got us through the tough days and the hard years. When we pray for our children, God reveals himself as our Way Maker, Miracle Worker, Promise Keeper, and Light Bringer. When love brings us to our knees in prayer, God shows up for us, and he shows up for our kids.

One of the things Josh and I know is this: God makes his presence felt when we pray for his help in the dark times. By 'dark times', we mean those seasons when life is so tough that you're tempted to give up all hope. Everyone goes through such valleys sooner or later. They are part and parcel of the human condition.

When I, Debra, got married, I was not a Christian. We're talking over four decades ago - March 1980, to be precise.

At the wedding service, my husband Frank and I decided to choose 'The Lord's my Shepherd' as one of our hymns. This is based on Psalm 23. One of the verses may be familiar to you:

Even though I walk
  through the darkest valley,
I will fear no evil,
  for you are with me,
your rod and your staff,
  they comfort me.

At the time, we had no real understanding of how important these words are, that God is reassuringly present when we walk through a vale of tears. Nor did we have any intuition that this timeless truth would be such a comfort in the years to come.

Like the time when Frank and I were leaders of a large church in South Manchester. Behind the scenes we were attending marriage counselling sessions because we were arguing with each other a lot. That was a difficult season. On entering the Relate marriage counselling building in Manchester, I met a member of our church who just happened to be there. I was so nervous about what they might think of me. As it turned out, they thought I was there to give some counselling, not receive it! This shows just how hard it was in those days to admit that you might need help if you were a person in church leadership. That said, God was present with us in the counselling. His rod and staff comforted us as we walked through the darkest of valleys, and things worked out just fine in the end. The fact that we've been married for forty years is proof of that. But at the time, we needed the Lord to be our Shepherd. It was a season of raw pain; we craved his comfort.

Then there was the time I was struggling as a mum. It was tough bringing up four children on a low budget and with a busy work schedule. I was overwhelmed, and I lost my temper. That was rare for me, so I felt such a bad example as a Christian. In desperation, I went for prayer ministry after a church service. The person praying for me was very kind. "There are things you might do better at," she said. "But there are lots of things you're also doing well. You're a good enough mum." What a comfort that was. Through her, God revealed himself as my Shepherd, the one who provides comfort when our eyes are filling. From then on, I found the idea of being a *good-enough* mother so liberating.[2] I had believed the lie that I needed to be perfect and had been living under great, self-imposed expectations. I now had to learn how to trust the Lord my Shepherd, and how to access his help in bringing up four children in a *good-enough* way.

Then there was the time when Josh, aged about five, became sick. The doctor thought it was a tummy bug, but in the middle of the night, Josh began crying out in pain. Thinking it might be appendicitis we rushed him to hospital. The following morning, a surgeon examined him. "He needs to go to surgery straightaway," he said. It was clear Josh was in danger. As we waited and waited during the operation, I called out to God. When Josh came out of theatre, we heard that his appendix had burst. It had been touch-and-go, but he was okay. The Shepherd was our comfort then too.

Finally, there were the long days, months, and years praying for Josh when he stopped showing any interest in church and started pursuing the things of this world. That was a tough time for us as parents. We watched him drift away until one night he was locked up in a Police cell. I was in the valley of the shadow, as he was, but God was our Shepherd again, as you'll see in this book.

SHOW ME YOUR WAYS

When you saw the word *Way Maker* on the cover, you might have been tempted to think that this book is all about the God who performs signs and wonders. Josh and I do believe that God can intervene in dramatic ways to transform our sickness into health, anxiety into contentment, darkness into light. We believe he really can give us an immediate and supernatural way out of suffering. We believe, in short, that God can act suddenly. But we also believe that God can act gradually. He can make his presence felt in our pain, giving us a sense that he is Immanuel, God with us. If in the first manifestation he is like a tsunami, in the second he is more like a rising tide. Both are equally valuable and valid, it's just that we tend to prefer stories of the sudden rather than gradual interventions of God. We prioritise testimonies that stress God's immense power over those about his comforting presence.

This brings me to why we have written this book. Many people seem to believe that God has only one way of operating, but he can reveal himself to us in so many ways. That's why Moses's prayer is so important – "Show me your ways" (Exodus 33:13). If the only way we think God can act is through sudden interventions, then in every dark season of our lives we will expect him to give us a quick way out of our difficulties. If that doesn't happen, we will almost certainly descend into a pit of disappointment. But if we understand from his Word that God isn't restricted to these kinds of interventions, then we will be okay with the fact that sometimes he doesn't extricate us from the valley of the shadow, but he lets us know he is walking with us through it. We need to learn to see God as more than just a Miracle Worker, marvellous though that is; we need to worship him as a Way Maker, Promise Keeper, and Light Bringer to use titles from 'Way Maker' by Sinach, a song that has been such a comfort to both Josh and me.[3]

MORE THAN A MIRACLE WORKER

That said, my story (Josh speaking now) is that God acted in my life through a dramatic intervention. The greatest miracle of all is when God takes us out of darkness into the kingdom of his light. I'm talking about salvation. I've been a Christian nearly two decades because my mother, among others, called out to God for my salvation. I experienced a miracle thanks to the prayers she and others prayed on my behalf. So, we're not doing a downer on dramatic interventions!

I grew up in a Christian family, going to church and loving most things I saw there. When I went to high school as a teenager, all that changed. I hadn't been hurt by church, nor had I experienced anything that made me angry with God. My parents ran a great church, and I had good friends there. There were young adults to look up to as role models and there was a strong sense of community. I often look back at these years and ask, why did I not choose to follow God?

The truth is, there is an intense spiritual battle over the soul and the salvation of every individual, and I was no exception. The Bible says that the god of this world has blinded the eyes of those who don't believe in Jesus (2 Corinthians 4:4). We don't see what a lifechanging difference Jesus will make if we follow him. That was me; I didn't see his beauty or his worth. I was much more enticed by the things of this world - friends, girls, partying, drinking, these were much more alluring to me. As for the Christian faith, my heart was apathetic.

Then I went through a very difficult time and ended up locked up in a police station. More on that later. There, Jesus brought about a dramatic turnaround in my life. In the run up to that, my parents must have thought the situation was hopeless. Only an encounter with Jesus could have saved and changed me. The good news is God has an amazing track record of being a Miracle Worker.

My story of coming to Jesus is a miracle, as is every salvation story, but it would be a mistake to say it only shows God as a Miracle Worker. That's like saying an author was only involved in writing the final act of a story, but not the acts that preceded it. Looking back, I know that God was involved in the build-up too. He was at work in the process not just in the crisis. He inspired people like my mother to pray in faith that God's promises would be fulfilled (Promise Keeper). He inspired many people to perform random acts of kindness that were like lights in the darkness (Light Bringer). And when I was arrested and put in a police cell, he found the most awe-inspiring way to get through to my hard heart (Way Maker). Our God is so much bigger and greater than a worker of wonders. His ways are many and mysterious.

I can track the glimpses of glory that led up to my transformation. There was what the Bible called a breaking up of the fallow ground of my heart. People were praying and, to use a Biblical picture, their prayers kept on filling the golden bowl in heaven until one day the bowl tipped and the blessings fell on me. God is in that phase too, not just the sudden revelation and dramatic transformation.

It is all too easy for Christian parents to feel guilty about the way they've parented. Like my mum in one of her examples above, we can begin to feel a failure and focus on our mistakes. The same is true for pastors and youth workers, and for Christian bosses and creatives. We create a one-size-fits-all picture of how God is supposed to work in our church, ministry, family, business, creativity, and then when it doesn't, we have a crisis of faith. But what if we conducted a deep-sea dive into the Bible and saw how infinitely multifaceted are God's ways? However much we want him to do 'a suddenly', God is not restricted to only being someone who performs miracles. He isn't confined to one story in our lives. His stories are many and marvellous.

My dad often says, "no seed is wasted." That's so true. However, we tend to focus on the climactic act of reaping rather than the long hard months of sowing. I want to honour the sowing season too - those times when my parents took me to youth events and exposed my ears to the message of Jesus and my eyes to the miracles he still performs. I remember going with Mum to conferences where I would help her run the bookstall. There I would also see the power of God at work. I remember being in church services and youth group meetings and those little seeds of faith being shared. God was making a way, fulfilling his promises, and shining his light before he worked a miracle. No seed was wasted in my life, and no seed will be wasted in your life either.

THE FOUR DESCRIPTIONS

As we wrap up this first chapter, we want to make a statement about what we believe concerning the ways of God.

We believe that God is a **Way Maker**, **Miracle Worker**, **Promise Keeper**, and **Light Bringer**. The Book of Isaiah Speaks wonderfully into these four themes.

First, he is a Way Maker. In Isaiah 43:2, God declares that he will be with us when we go through turbulence and trials.

When you pass through the waters,
 I will be with you;
and when you pass through the rivers,
 they will not sweep over you.
When you walk through the fire,
 you will not be burned;
 the flames will not set you ablaze.

Notice how God says **when**. He doesn't say **if**. We are going to go through difficult seasons. *When* we do, He will be with us, making a way *through* our troubles, not *around* them.

Secondly, he is indeed a Miracle Worker. In Isaiah 35-5-6, God says that when Messiah comes,

Then will the eyes of the blind be opened
  and the ears of the deaf unstopped.
Then will the lame leap like a deer,
  and the mute tongue shout for joy.
Water will gush forth in the wilderness
  and streams in the desert.

There will be dramatic and sudden transformations at every level. Sometimes, he will reveal that he is with us in our difficulties (Way Maker). At other times he will remove those difficulties from us supernaturally (Miracle Worker).

Thirdly, God is a Promise Keeper. He has made promises in his Word, and he loves it when his people are led by the Holy Spirit to a promise that he intends to fulfil in their lives. One of the greatest promises of God – one that has been cherished and declared by many who are hungry for a move of God - is in Isaiah 44:3:

I will pour water on the thirsty land,
  and streams on the dry ground;
I will pour out my Spirit on your offspring,
  and my blessing on your descendants.

When Mum was praying for me during my time away from God, she had to seize hold of God's promises in prayer. She had to appeal to God to be faithful to his promises – and with great results.

Fourthly, God is a Light Bringer who shines in the darkness

of this world through his people. As followers of Jesus, who is the Light of the World, we are called to be luminous. When we commit to being filled with the light of God's righteousness, we start to fulfil the Father's plan for us as his children. As it says in Isaiah 60:1-3:

Arise, shine, for your light has come,
*   and the glory of the Lord rises upon you.*
See, darkness covers the earth
*   and thick darkness is over the peoples,*
but the Lord rises upon you
*   and his glory appears over you.*
Nations will come to your light,
*   and kings to the brightness of your dawn.*

In the third and fourth revelations of God – as Promise Keeper and Light Bringer – we see God revealing his ways not just at the individual level (as he does as Way Maker and Miracle Worker) but at the societal level. God keeps his promise to pour out his Spirit on our community. God brings light to those who are oppressed and dispossessed. He is the one who brings light into the darkness of society. He loves us as individuals, but he also loves the world (John 3:16).

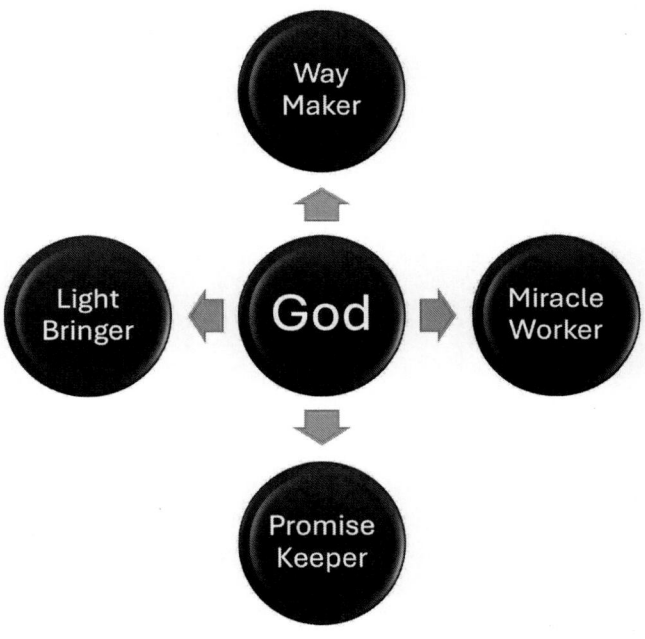

LET GOD BE GOD

This book is an exploration of the varied and wonderful ways in which God acts in our lives. It is designed in four parts corresponding to the four descriptions of God in Sinach's Way Maker song. In which of these do you need him to show up for you?

WAY MAKER

FOUR DESCRIPTIONS OF GOD	MY PRAYER FOR GOD TO ACT
WAY MAKER	Lord, as I pass through this time of difficulty, show me reassuring signs of your presence and your purposes in my life.
MIRACLE WORKER	Lord, as I face this challenging and perplexing situation, stretch out your mighty hand and do signs and wonders in my life.
PROMISE KEEPER	Lord, as I face what looks like an impossible situation, remind me of your promises, and that all things are possible with you.
LIGHT BRINGER	Lord, pour your light into my life and dispel every trace of darkness *in* me, then pour that light *through* me, so that others may see the light.

In the first part of our book, we're going to be looking at God as Way Maker. We're going to share from God's Word and from our own experience how we understand this awe-inspiring aspect of God's nature. Sometimes God's answer to our prayers involves him taking us *through* a difficulty rather than *around* it. If your calling is to go through a testing situation, our prayer is that God would reveal himself to you as your Way Maker. Sometimes God does use prevention as a tactic. But other times he chooses presence. Sometimes he takes us around a trial. Other times, he holds our hands and walks with us through it.

We believe that he is as much to be adored as our Way Maker as he is as our Miracle Worker.

Or our Promise Keeper.

Or Light Bringer.

In the end, we just need to let God be God.

He is sovereign.

Let him show up in the way he decides.

And rejoice when he does.

FOOTNOTES

1. *The Lincoln Year Book: Axioms and Aphorisms from the Great Emancipator* (ed. Library of Alexandria, 1907) - ISBN: 9781465522597.

2. Donald Winnicott – the pioneering British child psychologist - was the person who first came up with the phrase "good enough mother" in his book *Playing and Reality* (1953).

3. Sinach is a Nigerian Gospel singer. She issued Way Maker as a single in December 2015. A year later, she released a live album with the same song as the title track.

PART 1
WAY MAKER

CHAPTER 2
WALKING THROUGH FIRE (DEBRA)

It happened in the summer of 2023. I had just returned from speaking in Glasgow and was back at our headquarters in Manchester. Standing in the car park, I was engaged in a conversation with a church leader when, without warning, I suddenly felt as if someone had hit me on the head with a hammer. Later, I would be told that the correct term for this kind of episode is a "thunderclap".[1] People describe it as being more painful than childbirth.

"Are you alright?" the person asked.

"Fine."

That was a typical of me.

I wasn't.

When they left, I went and sat in my car. I was due to visit my dad who was poorly.

As I drove out of the car park, I nearly crashed. There was only one thing for it: I turned around, parked the car, and sat in the driver's seat, hoping whatever was ailing me would subside and disappear. But it didn't. The pain continued to be unbearable, and I now couldn't move. I knew this was serious.

Emma, our office cleaner, called my husband Frank. Within fifteen minutes he was sitting in the car next to me.

"I think I'm dying," I said. I followed this with trying to tell him all the things I wanted him to say to our kids and grandkids in case I didn't have the opportunity myself, but it was too painful to speak. It felt like my head was exploding.

"Let's hang on a minute and pray," he said. Even though I could see he was upset, he started calling out to God. At times like this, Frank is the very best person to have around. He's so calm.

But the pain didn't subside.

Worse still, I was violently sick. Since I couldn't even move my head, my dress ended up covered. Despite this, and the thought that I might be at death's door, I wasn't at any point afraid. Remember what I said about Psalm 23 in the last chapter? I might have been walking through the valley of the shadow of death, but I wasn't living at that moment from a place of fear. I knew my Shepherd was with me. His rod and staff still comforted me. I was at peace.

Frank called 111 from my phone and answered routine questions, explaining my symptoms as best as he could.

"Is she breathing?"

"Yes."

"Is she conscious?"

"Yes."

So, it went on.

"We'll have an ambulance to you as soon as we can, but it

may be three to four hours."

Frank was later to tell me how scared he was at this point. So many questions flooded his mind. How long would the ambulance take? Had he answered the questions accurately? How could he get me out of my seat and rush me into hospital? He didn't show it, but I now know how worried he was.

Just a few minutes later, my phone rang. It was my GP calling from St John's medical practice in Altrincham.

"Have you called 111?"

Frank told her about his conversation.

"Is Debra with you now?"

"Yes."

"Please step out of the car so she can't hear."

Frank told me later what she said.

"From the symptoms you've described, I'm 99% sure she's had a brain bleed. I'm upgrading your status. The ambulance will be with you in twenty minutes, not three-to-four hours."

She was true to her word.

When the ambulance arrived, it took me straight to Salford Royal Hospital.

Frank came with me.

"Why are we heading to Salford?" Frank asked.

"It just popped up on my screen," the driver replied. "I expected Wythenshawe," he continued. "Salford's just a computer-generated selection based on capacity and waiting times." What we didn't know at the time was that Salford is one of the finest neurological hospitals in the UK. I was on my way to the best place for my condition. Even though the ride was bumpy, I had been given pain relief. I was at peace.

Once we had arrived at the hospital, I had a CT scan. This confirmed I had a brain bleed, also known as a brain haemorrhage – bleeding between the brain tissue and the skull, or inside the brain tissue. This is a life-threatening condition that requires immediate medical attention. Brain haemorrhages – or haemorrhagic strokes – are caused by bleeding in and around the brain. They are generally more severe than strokes caused by a blockage. Around one third of patients don't survive longer than a month, and many who do survive are left with lifelong disabilities. It was a good thing my GP had upgraded the ambulance call. Time was of the essence.

One of the staff informed me I would be having an operation the next morning, August 10th, 2023.

"There are two main surgical techniques to treat subdural haematomas. The first is craniotomy where a section of the skull is temporarily removed so the haematoma can be accessed and removed. A small burr hole is drilled into the skull and a tube is inserted through the hole to help drain the haematoma."

I already knew I preferred the second.

"The second is 'coiling' which involves approaching the aneurysm from inside the blood vessel, so there's no need to open the skull. Small metal coils are inserted into the aneurysm through the arteries that run from the groin to the brain. The coils remain in the aneurysm. They are not removed."

My surgeon chose the second.

The next morning, a golden thread was used to access the aneurysm, and the procedure was successful. It had been quite an ordeal, but at least I could say I had gold in my brain!

By now, thanks to the power of social media, I had thousands of people praying for my recovery. Sadly, I couldn't read all the get-well messages until much later because I had to lie flat for around a week and keep my head perfectly still.

It was while I was lying in bed that I heard Sinach's worship song called 'Way Maker.' I thought it was coming from my phone, but I discovered it was playing over the hospital radio. As soon as I heard it, I felt so comforted. I knew I was going to be okay.

"That's a lovely song," I said to a nurse.

She replied, "I've never heard them play it before."

God had shown up as my Way Maker. He had made a way where there was no way.

News began to spread of how God had answered our prayers. It travelled so far that my friend Les Moir told us it even reached Sinach. She was over the moon that her song had helped me so much, as was I. I just lay in my bed during those days, crying over the goodness of God in speaking to me through that song. The timing of it was amazing. To me it was a sign. Often, we can't see God's presence, but right then I knew that God was with me, closer than ever. I knew he was working in my life and that I would survive.

During these days, I was visited by our four adult children who told me how much I meant to them which was very moving to hear. It's sad that we often only say these things in life-threatening situations, although Josh tells me he says them more frequently than that! I'm sure the others would say the same.

Demonstrations of God's kindness continued. A friend from twenty-plus years ago appeared at my bedside. She is a senior registrar at Salford Royal. She walked in with fresh coffee, orange juice, croissants, and other goodies. The following day another friend who worked at the hospital came bearing gifts and then a third person came. Hospital staff who knew me kept arriving with gifts. Okay, I have a lot of friends, and some are medics. I suppose it's forty years of attending churches, conferences, and knowing a lot of people.

"Are you someone special?" the lady in the bed next to mine asked. Others were curious. "Are you famous? Do you work here?"

During these seven days, I was told to keep completely still as I lay on my bed. I wasn't even permitted to sit up, which meant I had to use my phone lying down. This led to me finding ways to pass the time. We had recently moved house, and we needed bunkbeds for our grandchildren. I started to look on Google, but I wanted advice. I put a post on Facebook to ask my friends. Someone replied with a stern one-word imperative, "Rest!" I started looking for a bunkbed retailer by that name until I realised that I was being reprimanded for not relaxing - not advice I find easy to follow.

Before leaving the hospital, I had to take a memory test. This required following a nurse to another ward, going into the kitchen, and making a cup of tea with one sugar. I then had to find my way back to my ward without any assistance. It was a bit basic but following simple instructions can be hard when you've had a brain injury. Thankfully I passed and was told it was nearly time to go home.

I had one big thing on my mind at this point. It was our daughter's wedding on Saturday August 26th. I was desperate to be there, especially since I was meant to be the celebrant. On Tuesday August 22nd I was sent home with my drugs and told to rest. On the day, I felt well enough to go to the wedding. It was wonderful being there. People kept saying I was a walking miracle. But it was God who had made a way.

THERE MAY BE TROUBLE AHEAD

The seeds for this book were sown during those moments when the song 'Way Maker' was playing in the hospital. As I listened, I was reminded of how God makes a way for us through our trials. At the beginning of Isaiah chapter 43, we read:

> *Now this is what the Lord says -*
> *he who created you, Jacob,*
> *he who formed you, Israel:*
> *"Do not fear, for I have redeemed you;*
> *I have summoned you by name; you are mine.*
> *When you pass through the waters,*
> *I will be with you;*
> *and when you pass through the rivers,*
> *they will not sweep over you.*
> *When you walk through the fire,*
> *you will not be burned;*
> *the flames will not set you ablaze.*

A few verses later (16-19), God also makes this wonderful declaration about who he is and what he's doing:

This is what the Lord says—
* he who made a way through the sea,*
* a path through the mighty waters,*
who drew out the chariots and horses,
* the army and reinforcements together,*
and they lay there, never to rise again,
* extinguished, snuffed out like a wick:*
"Forget the former things;
* do not dwell on the past.*
See, I am doing a new thing!
* Now it springs up; do you not perceive it?*
I am making a way in the wilderness
* and streams in the wasteland.*

You'll notice the use of the word "way." Our God makes a way through the sea, through rivers, through deep waters, and through fire. He makes a way for us in the wilderness and provides streams in the wasteland. I'm sure you realise these are pictures from Israel's history. They remind us of Israel passing through the Red Sea and their wanderings in the desert. They remind us of the three faithful Hebrews who went into the fiery furnace in Babylon and were not consumed. These echoes from Israel's past are used to reinforce one simple point, that when we pass through times of great testing, we are not alone. Just as a fourth man appeared in the fiery furnace – one who was clearly more than a man – so God is with us when we pass through the fire. With God in your life, the Liverpool anthem (sorry Frank and Josh!) takes on a completely different meaning: "You'll never walk alone." Why? Because as Isaiah 43:2 says, "I will be with you."

WALKING THROUGH FIRE (DEBRA)

YOU CAN'T GO ROUND

Saving Private Ryan is one of the most brutal war films ever made. It tells the story of Captain Miller and his band of soldiers who are given the task of finding a certain Private Ryan. His three brothers have been killed in action in different parts of the world and the US high command back home decide that the last remaining brother should be tracked down and returned to his mother. The prospect of her losing all four of her sons is not one they're prepared to countenance. So, off Captain Miller (Tom Hanks) goes to find the man.

After a terrifying landing on Omaha Beach, Miller and his men head inland to search for the soldier. At one point, they walk into a field where there are several dead cows. It becomes obvious that these animals have been cut down by enemy machine-gun fire. Miller, looking through his binoculars, sees a defensive position on the crest of a small hill about three hundred metres ahead of them. There is a machine gun protecting a radio station on the elevated land. Miller tells his men to prepare to attack the enemy gunners ahead of them.

"Can't we go around it?" the men ask.

Miller shakes his head. "If we don't deal with it, some poor platoon will walk right into their line of fire."

The men understand their officer's reasoning, but they are still reluctant. The weather is gloomy and there's a sense of foreboding in the air. Even so, they prepare their weapons and take off their back packs, ready for a dangerous charge up the hill.

What happens next is as vivid and traumatic as anything

else in the film. They take the position, but one of their men – the medic – is shot in the stomach and dies slowly. The loss hits the men hard, and Captain Miller is forced to exercise extraordinary leadership skills to get their minds back into alignment with the mission.

YOU'VE GOT TO GO THROUGH

What's this got to do with Isaiah 43? A lot, as it happens. In Isaiah 43, God says to his people, "When you walk through the fire". There are three very important words there. The first one to underline is "through." As human beings, we all have a natural desire and inclination to want to go *around* our difficulties. Rather than go through the tough and challenging experiences of life, we would like to go past them, keeping our heads down, making sure that the enemy doesn't see us and the dangers don't touch us. This is very understandable. We are all pain averse. If we can avoid suffering, we will go to almost any lengths to do so. But this isn't always possible. Some situations need to be gone *through* not *around*. As the old saying goes, a smooth sea does not make a skilful mariner. Only storms can do that. Likewise, a comfortable and challenge-free life does not make a mature Christian. Passing through rivers and walking through fire does.

So, the first life lesson to pull from Isaiah 43 is this: God's ways are not our ways. Sometimes, we must go *through* situations, not *around* them. This is because we learn things about God and ourselves in a crisis that we can never learn in comfort.

The second thing we learn is that these 'dark times' are going to be experienced by all of us. Notice, the verse does not say *if* you pass through the rivers, or *if* you walk through the fire. It says *when*. As much as we would love to hear otherwise, God does not always snatch us out of times of trouble and testing. What is it Jesus promised his disciples in John 16? He said, "in the world you will have trouble!" I don't hear many claiming that promise when they pray! God's Word warns us we're going to fly through turbulence. But listen to what Jesus adds. "Fear not. I have overcome the world!" Jesus makes a way where there is no way. He is the overcomer. He is bigger than any storm.

It's important to say that this does not mean God won't sometimes perform mighty works of power in which our sicknesses are snatched away and our poverty replaced by abundance. God can do this too because he does miracles, he doesn't just make a way for us. It's just that any claim that this is always his will needs to be modified in the light of passages like Isaiah 43. God promises us that we will go *through* the valley of the shadow of death. Jesus promises that in the world we will experience 'trouble'. As much as we would love to see nothing but idyllic landscapes ahead of us, there are machine gun posts hidden by the trees, and it's not a matter of *if* we run into them, it's *when*.

So, the second life lesson to pull from these words is this: it's only a matter of time before you stumble upon a river or come across a fire. You're not facing them because God loves you less than those who are enjoying God's favour. Everyone goes through these rivers and fires. No one is immune or exempt from these experiences.

Thirdly, notice the word *walk*. Isaiah 43 talks about us *walking* through the fire. I don't know about you, but if I was in a conflagration of any kind, my natural inclination would be to run as fast as possible out of that location. But God tells us to *walk*. The British evangelist and author Alan Redpath has something encouraging and insightful to say about the use of this word. "Walking is the pace at which you go when you are not in a hurry, when you are not concerned or alarmed. When you are not burdened or anxious, then you walk. 'He that believeth shall not make haste' (Isaiah 28:16)."[2]

So, the third life lesson is this: go through challenging seasons at a pace that allows you to maximise the learning potential of every precious second. In the Psalms, David often thanks God for the afflictions he endures because they teach him new truths (Psalm 119:50, 67, 71). We should do the same.

PREVENTION AND PRESENCE

It's important to understand the difference between God as a Way Maker and God as a Miracle Worker. If we're honest, we would all prefer God to show up by doing wonders whenever we are faced with serious and even life-threatening situations. When a person is told they have a serious illness, it is natural for them to pray, "Lord Jesus, stretch out your mighty hand and do a miracle in my life!" When a person needs to raise a lot of money to fund a huge building project, it's normal for them to pray, "Lord, do a miracle!" When we face immense difficulties, we long for God to reveal himself as our Miracle Worker and to remove every great obstacle and difficulty. But sometimes God's purpose is not to show up in a dramatic and sudden way. Sometimes he wants to walk slowly with us through our pain.

What we're talking about here is the difference between prevention and presence. Human beings are allergic to pain. This means that our instinctive reflex is to want to pass around it or be lifted out of it before it consumes our lives. This encourages us to pursue a theology of prevention. "Oh God, prevent me from suffering this ordeal. Do something mighty, marvellous, and miraculous. Remove me from the dark time that's ahead of me." This kind of prayer resembles Captain Kirk in the original Star Trek series. It's a religious version of his "Beam me up Scotty" – a request often made in the face of impending danger. I'm not disrespecting this tendency nor dismissing this prayer. It's as natural to us as feeling hungry or desiring sleep. Even Jesus exhibited this understandable longing to avoid suffering. When he was in the Garden Gethsemane, he prayed, "Abba, Father, everything is possible for you. Take this cup from me" (Mark 14:36). But then he added, "Yet not what I will, but what you will."

Sometimes, however, prevention is not the right plan for us. Sometimes, we need to walk with God *through* the valley of the shadow. Sometimes we need to draw comfort from the small but comforting signs that he is with us. Sometimes, in short, we need to be satisfied with his presence rather than crave his prevention.

Before launching his own organisation, Gen Zeal, Josh spent three years working for 24-7 Prayer, an international prayer movement founded by Pete Greig. Pete has a very helpful analogy for what we're talking about here. He teaches that there are basically two ways in which God answers our prayers for help.³ The first he describes as an *airlift*. This is when God comes and takes us out of a situation of great difficulty. It involves a display of his power, so we can justly say that it showcases God as Miracle Worker. The second response is what he calls *parachuting in*. This is when God does not airlift us out of a crisis but rather releases his resources to us, the most important of which is of course his presence. If the first involves us being taken out of our afflictions, the second involves him drawing alongside us in our difficulties. It involves comforting signs of his presence, so we can justly say that it showcases God as Way Maker.

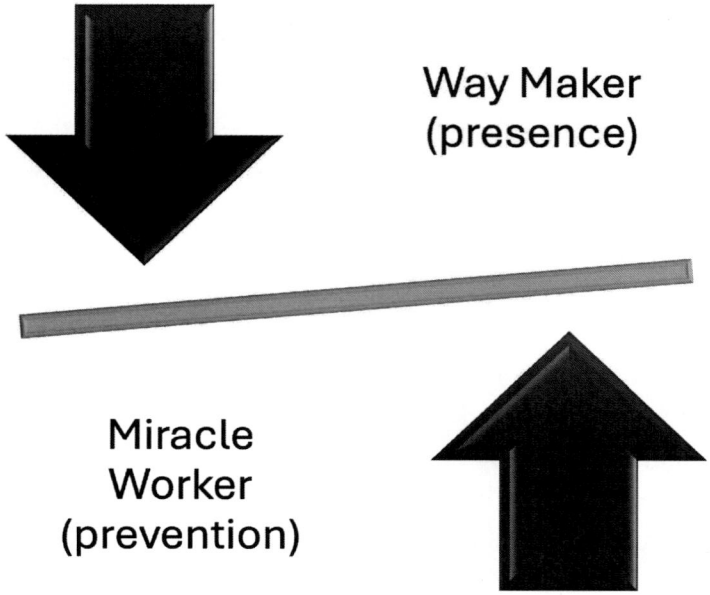

WALKING THROUGH FIRE (DEBRA)

LIGHTNING BOLTS AND FIREFLIES

In the last chapter I wrote about how important Psalm 23 has been in my life. That passage compares God to a loving shepherd who leads his sheep through dark valleys. When it's very dark and the sheep cannot see him, the shepherd walks ahead of his flock and uses his staff to hit the rocks nearby. The sound of this light tap-tapping encourages the sheep that he is showing them the way. It's a very reassuring picture because there are seasons of our lives when things seem quite dark and perplexing, and in those times it's easy for us to miss the sights and sounds of his presence. We would love in those difficulties for God to act in an awe-inspiring and dramatic way, lifting us out of a pitch-black valley and placing us on a sunny mountaintop. But he knows what's best for us, and he does not always show up in that way. We ask for him to reveal himself to us in miracles, but he chooses to come to us as our comforter and companion. When there's low spiritual visibility, he taps the rocks to reassure us that he's nearby.

There are few things more sudden and dramatic in nature than bolts of lightning. In the Bible, lightning is associated with God's mighty power. We see lightning when God gives the ten commandments to his people. "On the morning of the third day there was thunder and lightning, with a thick cloud over the mountain, and a very loud trumpet blast. Everyone in the camp trembled. Then Moses led the people out of the camp to meet with God, and they stood at the foot of the mountain" (Exodus 19:16-17). We see lightning at the end of the Bible when John has a vision of God's throne in heaven.

"From the throne came flashes of lightning, rumblings and peals of thunder" (Revelation 4:5). Jesus' second coming is likened to a lightning bolt: "For as lightning that comes from the east is visible even in the west, so will be the coming of the Son of Man" (Matthew 24:27).

Lightning bolts are impressive. Bright flashes of light that descend from the heavens to the earth, they are a striking metaphor of those moments when God invades our suffering and reveals his awe-inspiring power. Lightning is therefore a useful metaphor when we come to think of God as the Miracle Worker. But fireflies are impressive too - not in the way lightning is, of course, but they still take our breath away. If you're out at twilight and you see these light-emitting beetles rising from the marshes into the night sky, this also evokes wonder - not a wonder that makes you tremble with shock (as lightning does), but a wonder that makes you tingle with serenity. There is something reassuring about these tiny airborne lanterns brightening the night and lighting the way. If the lightning bolt reveals God as Miracle Worker, the firefly reveals him as Way Maker. If the lightning bolts encourage us to praise, the fireflies encourage us to persevere.

A STILL, SMALL VOICE

You'd think that I would want to end this chapter in praise of lightning bolts, given that I suffered a medical episode known as a thunderclap. But this is not the case at all. I believe that God can do mighty and sudden works, yes. But I also believe that there are times when we need to be alert to far less dramatic manifestations – to the soft tapping of his staff, the silent lights in the night. These are the sounds and sights that reveal him as our Way Maker.

Sometimes it's very hard to make these out while we are going through difficulties. God's sounds and sights can be so imperceptible that they are only seen later, as we look back on what we've experienced and have those aha moments. "He was there!" "He was present!" "He was closer to me than I ever realised!" Sometimes it is only in retrospect that we recognise that God was passing with us through the river, walking with us through the fire.

To hear the tapping of God's rod and staff, sometimes we need to cease our haste and drown out the noise. Remember Elijah? He was terrified and depressed, desperately in need of God's intervention. He went up the same mountain where God had spoken to Moses through the thunder and lightning and stood there waiting for God to speak to him. He was desperate to hear God's voice. God subsequently passed him in a hurricane, in an earthquake, and in the flash and fire of lightning, but Elijah didn't hear him in any of these demonstrations of raw power. It was only when the prophet stilled his racing heart that he heard God, but it was in a low whisper, a still, small voice (1 Kings 19).

If you and I want to have a revelation of God as our Way Maker, we need to be prepared to go through seasons of difficulty and testing situations. How are we ever going to see God make a way where there is no way unless we find ourselves in a situation where there seems to be little hope, poor prospects, little visibility? It's only when we pass through the turbulent waters of relationship challenges and walk through blazing flames of personal attacks that God can show that he is our Way Maker. If we never get our feet wet and never feel the heat, how can God show himself to us in this beautiful and remarkable manner? If our beliefs say that he must always airlift us before we face the currents and the flames, then we will never get to see how he walks with us in our troubles, nor will we ever learn to discern how to hear his still small voice and grow as sons and daughters of God. Put another way, if we are obsessed with lightning, what chance have we of ever seeing the fireflies rising in the sky?

When I was lying in that hospital bed, I heard the song, 'Way Maker'. The revelation of God as our Way Maker was what I needed while I was recovering from surgery. As soon as I heard those lyrics and that melody, there wasn't just gold in my brain, there was gold in my soul – the gold of God's Way Maker revelation.

When we are in the valley of the shadow, he walks where we walk. He goes ahead of us, tapping on the rocks, making a way. If you're experiencing great challenges and difficulties right now, trust that God is in control of the process. I quoted Alan Redpath a few pages ago, and I'm going to quote him again. "There is nothing - no circumstance, no trouble, no testing - that can ever touch me until, first of all, it has gone past God and past Christ right through to me. If it has come that far, it has come with a great purpose, which I may not understand at the moment. But as I refuse to become panicky, as I lift up my eyes to Him and accept it as coming from the throne of God for some great purpose of blessing to my own heart, no sorrow will ever disturb me, no circumstance will cause me to fret, for I shall rest in the joy of what my Lord is - that is the rest of victory!"[4]

Amen to that! Just remember, always your Way Maker and sometimes your Miracle Worker. And if anyone knows how to make a way where there is no way, it is the one who is called 'the Way,' and whose followers were originally called the People of the Way.

So, if you're in a bed on a hospital ward worried about your health, or you're waiting to apply for benefits in a depressing waiting room, or you're standing in a crematorium saying goodbye to someone you have loved and lost, look for tiny tokens of the Way Maker's presence. He has made you a promise. When you walk through the fire, or you pass through the rivers, he says this:

I WILL BE WITH YOU.

FOOTNOTES

1. "A thunderclap headache is an extremely painful headache that comes on suddenly, like a clap of thunder. This type of headache has the most intense pain at its onset. People who have had a thunderclap headache often describe it as the worst headache of their life, unlike any headache they've ever experienced. Thunderclap headaches strike without any warning. Sometimes there's no underlying medical cause to them, but other times they're a sign of very serious underlying conditions that involve bleeding in and around your brain. This type of headache is rare. They occur in less than 50 out of 100,000 adults each year. It's important to seek medical attention immediately to rule out life-threatening causes of a thunderclap headache." See "Thunderclap Headaches" entry on www.my.clevelandclinic.org

2. Alan Redpath, *Captivity to Conquest: Studies in the Prophecy of Isaiah, chapters 40-66* (1978) – originally published as *Faith for the Times*.

3. On X (formerly Twitter), Pete Greig said this, "We want God to airlift us out of our problems, but more often than not, He parachutes in and joins us in the midst of them" (24.03.2018). He also talks about this in his book *God on Mute: Engaging the Silence of Unanswered Prayer, p 219 & 336*.

4. Alan Redpath. https://billmuehlenberg.com/2022/11/05/notable-christians-alan-redpath/

CHAPTER 3
THE PRAYER GOD ALWAYS ANSWERS (JOSH)

I'll never forget that day. Two things happened; one was a miracle, the other a mystery. The miracle was seeing hundreds of young people come to Jesus. That was awesome. The mystery was hearing Mum had been rushed to hospital two hundred miles away with a life-threatening condition. That wasn't awesome. It was awful.

I remember the phone call as if it was yesterday. Even though the signal was terrible, I could hear my dad fighting back the tears as he tried to communicate that Mum's situation was touch-and-go. Some of my friends could tell I was receiving bad news. They were mouthing, "Is everything okay?" I mouthed back, "Not really," trying to keep everything together in a very Stoic, British way while wondering if my mum was going to die.

Dad explained that I couldn't go to the hospital yet. "There's nothing any of us can do except pray," he said.

In times like these, we have two choices - to allow the pain to paralyse us into prayerlessness or to run into the arms of our heavenly Father and start praying. I've learned the hard way that not praying keeps us from knowing his comfort and healing. It prevents us from benefiting from all the spiritual lessons we can only learn when life is more complex than comfortable. So many times, I've heard people say, "I don't know how I could've got through that without God." I can only respond with an empathetic, "Amen." When life serves up mysteries rather than miracles, there are priceless truths to learn. When I remember to lean into Jesus during the dark times, I find him close, comforting, and compassionate.

Praying can pave the way for miracles, but it can also help us receive comfort in the face of mystery, when miracles don't happen. When we pray, we sometimes see God move in wonderful ways, performing miracles of salvation, healing, and deliverance. In these dramatic moments, we witness demonstrations of God's power which evoke awe. At other times, it can feel as if God is not answering our prayers, at least not in the way we expect. As we will see in a later chapter, in the first instance, God seems to say, "Yes, I'll do it now." In the second, he seems to say, "I'll do it, but not yet," or "I'm making a way. Hang in there!" In the first case, everything seems as clear as a sunny day. In the second, it feels as dark as a moonless night. Just to add to the complexity, sometimes we witness these things at the same time, like when I saw hundreds come to Jesus while hearing my mum had been rushed to hospital, her life on the line.

MIRACLE AND MYSTERY

Six months after this happened to Mum, my dear father-in-law died of cancer on the same day I was set to embark on a national tour calling young people to pray for revival.

We had visited our beloved Dave, my wife's father, at the hospice. We knew he only had days to live, but we didn't expect him to pass as soon as he did. While my wife Emma and I were sound asleep, Emma's father was reunited in heaven with her mother Sandra who we had lost years before. The next morning, we woke up to find missed calls and texts from the hospice and from Emma's family. They had been desperately trying to contact us as we slept. Looking back, I see God's hand in this. The gift of that night's sleep was a small, firefly-sized hint of God's presence with us.

The shock of Dave's death was so intense that for a few hours I forgot that my grandad's funeral was taking place later that same day. I'll never forget my final moments with my precious grandad – my mum's dad. Trembling from the effects of Parkinson's, he squeezed my hand as tight as he could and stared into my eyes. "Never let go or lose sight of the Word of God," he said. What a brief beam of light in the darkness that was. To his dying day, my grandad was deeply committed to the Scriptures, probably more than anyone else I have ever known. What a legacy he left in our lives.

And here's the point I want to make - we would have loved God to reveal himself by doing a healing miracle in the lives of my father-in-law and my grandad, but God manifested himself differently from that, showing that he was walking with them and with us in the valley of the shadow, tapping on the rocks with his shepherd's staff, releasing fireflies into the darkness. Whenever we walk through the valley of the shadow, what we truly need are signs that our loving heavenly Father is with us in our pain. We long for an "ever-present help in time of need" (Psalm 46:1), a "wonderful counsellor" (Isaiah 9:6), someone to "lead us beside still waters" (Psalm 23:2) and to restore our souls. We have such a person: Jesus, the Way Maker.

Our natural inclination in times of mystery and confusion is to ask the question why. Why are these things happening to me? Why is God allowing me to suffer? Why does a God of love not prevent me from experiencing pain? However understandable these questions are – and I've asked them many times - I am not sure these are the most productive. Perhaps it would be better to ask *where* more than *why* – not why does a God of love allow us to suffer pain – a question that has challenged theologians for millennia - but *where* is God when his children go through the valley of death?

One thing I am sure of is that God is with us. He is not distant and unconcerned; he is intimately present and profoundly affected by the testing times we endure here on earth. He walks where we walk. He feels what we feel. He is Immanuel, God with us. He is not God against us, or God absent from us. He is God among us. He understands. Put another way, the God revealed in Jesus is not apathetic when we suffer pain. He is sympathetic. Better still, he is empathetic. He suffers with us. This is the God revealed by Jesus, and this is the God I've had to cling to as I have walked a sometimes twisting path of mystery rather than a clear highway of miracles.

PRESENCE AND PRESENTS

I guess this could sound too good to be true, especially if you're in the middle of a storm as you read this. Remember how Jesus slept peacefully while his disciples were panicking on a boat? Jesus - the Prince of Peace - was with those frightened men. I'm convinced he wants us to know that he is present with us as we pass through the storms. It's the awareness of his presence we need to pray for when the waves are high. When we know he is with us, panic is replaced by peace.

If you're in any doubt about this, listen to what Jesus taught these same disciples about prayer in Luke 11:

"Which of you fathers, if your son asks for a fish, will give him a snake instead? Or if he asks for an egg, will give him a scorpion? If you then, though you are evil, know how to give good gifts to your children, how much more will your Father in heaven give the Holy Spirit to those who ask him!"

Notice how Jesus doesn't say "good gifts" in the promise he makes. He says, "the Holy Spirit."[1] In this passage, Jesus says that God wants to give us his presence not his presents. When it comes to more trivial matters, we often think we know what we need, and so we present a shopping list of these needs to God, asking him to give us specific blessings and gifts. But while these may be good, they may not necessarily be the best – in other words, what we truly need. The same is true for the more painful times when we pray and don't get the answer we want. It's in these times we can discover, if we push deeper into prayer, that God's best is oftentimes not what comes from his hands but what shines from his face. When we are going through the valley of the shadow, God promises simply to be with us. This is the conclusion of Jesus' teaching on prayer in Luke 11. "My presence is with you in your hour of need." There is therefore a prayer that God always answers with a yes – the prayer for his presence. This is the ultimate gift.

Some may say, isn't God always present? According to the Bible, he is omnipresent – present everywhere. Sometimes, however, we can become unconscious of his presence. We don't always sense it, or we may have a limited framework for understanding the ways he makes his presence felt. Remember, the Bible portrays many ways in which God's presence is made manifest: a thundering voice and a gentle whisper, a guiding shepherd and a blazing pillar of fire, still waters and earthquakes, green pastures and burning mountains. We need to recognise these multifaceted divine ways.

We also need to encounter in our hearts what we know in our heads. If our thoughts tell us he must be present, because the Bible tells us so (Psalm 139), our feelings need to catch up with that truth so we can experience this divine reality in a personal and heartfelt way. So, the prayer that God always loves to answer is "Make me more aware of your presence." That's our greatest need.

When I pray this prayer, there are many things he shows me, but the overriding message is that he is with me. It's as if my heavenly Father is reassuring me that whatever I'm going through, he is with me on the way. He says,

My child, you are not alone.
I am with you.
I will never leave you.
I have walked this road before.
I am walking it with you now.
I will walk it with you in the future.
I am the Way.
You are a child of the Way.
Let me make the way clear to you.
I am your Way Maker.
I make a way where there is no way.

It's like the meditation called 'Footprints.'[2] When we look back, we see something puzzling in the sand behind us. In the good times, there are two sets of footprints – one set belongs to us, the other to Jesus. But when times of suffering come, only one set is visible. Why? Because in those seasons, Jesus carried us. He held and upheld us when the thunder roared, the wind howled, and the waves boomed. He forged a path for us through mystery and adversity. He was and always will be the one who makes a way where there seems to be no way.

WHEN MIRACLES DON'T HAPPEN

Why do miracles not always happen? In a sense, this is a strange question to ask. Miracles are, by definition, exceptional events which leave us reeling with wonder. If they happened often, they would fail to be exceptional and they would therefore no longer fill us with awe. Ask yourself some questions. How many chapters are there in the Book of Acts? The answer is 28. How many years of the Church's earliest history does the Book of Acts cover? The answer is approximately 30. How many individual miracles are described in those 30 years? The answer is approximately 30. That's only one a year.

When you read the Book of Acts, you can sometimes forget that there were so few because Luke, the author, leaves out days, weeks, and months when nothing extraordinary was happening. This is how storytellers work. They don't describe what's mundane and boring; they leave that out and focus on what's important. Luke does precisely this in the Book of Acts. We know he researched meticulously before he wrote his story of the acts of the apostles. I'm sure there was a lot that he chose not to include. By omitting all this, he gave us the impression that the apostles were performing miraculous acts all the time. But this is not the case. Miracles are rare.[3] If they weren't, we'd all get 'awed out' and stop being amazed when they happened.

So, what do we do when the miracle we're so desperately longing for doesn't happen? I'd like to suggest three things.

1. Seek Him in the Mystery

We need to understand that God is, well, God! He's beyond our limited human comprehension. So, when we ask questions like this, we're diving into the complexities of the nature of God. It's important to remember that God longs for relationship with us; he is a Being that is to be known relationally more than he is to be understood academically. So, while we can love and know him, any idea we might have that we are going to fully comprehend him in this life is one we should reject.

There's a very good reason why this is the case. If our finite minds could grasp everything there was to know about God's infinite wisdom, then there's a very real sense in which God will have ceased to be God. Why? Because if I can understand everything there is to understand about an infinite and all-wise God, then my mind is greater than God.

Andy Mineo, a popular Christian rapper from USA, says, "The opposite of faith isn't doubt. It's when I've got it all figured out."[4] No wonder our lives sometimes take us down roads that seem misty rather than clear. Mystery, then, should be embraced as a normal part of the Christian life. It might even be necessary, especially if our faith is only truly tested during times of suffering. A sword will never be sharp enough for the battle unless it is first forged in a furnace of fire.

One of the pastors at the church Mum and I attend - Ramp Church, Manchester – is called Joe Reeser. He talks about God as a heavenly Father who plays hide and seek with us. Sometimes, like an earthly father, he conceals himself from us to promote a longing in us to seek him. People have known this about God for thousands of years. The prophet Isaiah declared in Isaiah 45:15, "Truly, you are the God who hides himself." God does this because he wants to see just how hungry we are for his presence. Are we a people who seek him with our whole hearts? Do we long to see his face? I like the idea of playing hide and seek with my heavenly Father. There is joy in that picture. It conveys a deep relationship rather than one of distance (even though God can feel faraway at certain times). And there is something profound about this thought – that the seeking is supposed to be as important and as lifegiving as the finding.

If we seek God in the mysterious times, we'll start to see that his timing is perfect, his truth is timeless, his grace is sufficient, his wisdom is marvellous (although also mysterious), and his ways are higher than ours. Remember what Isaiah 55:8-9 says:

> *"For my thoughts are not your thoughts,*
> *neither are your ways my ways,"*
> *declares the Lord.*
> *"As the heavens are higher than the earth,*
> *so are my ways higher than your ways*
> *and my thoughts than your thoughts."*

God calls us to pursue him. Let's not allow a lack of clarity on our part to stop us encountering him. Rather, let's allow our inability to see him clearly to drive us to look a little closer.

2. Recall God's History

God has a track record, in the Bible and in our own lives, of showing he can and does do miracles. This can pose a problem when we're hoping for a breakthrough, but it seems to be delayed. That's where recalling God's faithfulness in the past helps us to know for sure that his ways are good. Just as David recalled his victories against the lion and the bear as he prepared to fight Goliath, so we too should recall God's history of faithfulness as we prepare to step into the next stage of his calling on our lives. Sometimes we know this in theory but struggle to believe it in our hearts, especially when God's plan seems to make no sense. But as we remind ourselves of God's goodness in the past, it fills us with hope for the future. Our trust in him them begins to transfer from our heads to our hearts. This strengthens our resolve to walk the journey God has carved out for us no matter how difficult.

Jesus promised that we would know 'another Comforter' (John 14:16). When he said 'another', he meant 'another Comforter like me.' When he said 'Comforter', he used a special and specific word. You may have heard the word Paraclete before.[5] This is the word translated Comforter. It literally means 'someone called alongside to help you.' Again, think of the famous *Footprints* meditation. Have you ever known a time when you were going through real difficulties? In those times, did you experience heavenly peace? That's the Paraclete – the Comforter. The Comforter Jesus was referring to is the Holy Spirit.

When God's Spirit draws alongside us in our pain, he brings consolation. In his manifest presence, we feel the peace of God – a peace that the world cannot give. If you encounter mystery rather than a miracle, spend time in the Comforter's presence. This is one of the primary purposes of the presence of God, to comfort us in our trials. The personal, powerful and active presence of God is available for all believers, young and old. It is the source of the great strength we so often need to walk the way God has made for us. How encouraging that God not only makes a path through the difficulties of life but also gives us the power to walk it.

3. Fight from God's Victory

We sometimes can forget that God has already defeated the enemy. Jesus conquered sin and death through his death and resurrection. This means that we do not have to win that battle all over again in prayer. Rather, our responsibility is to bring the already-secured victory of God to bear in the troubling situations we are facing. Paul is very clear about this in Ephesians 1:20-22: "He raised Christ from the dead and seated him at his right hand in the heavenly realms, far above all rule and authority, power and dominion, and every name that is invoked, not only in the present age but also in the one to come. And God placed all things under his feet." In Ephesians 2:6, he reminds us that we are seated with Christ in these heavenly places.

Why, then, does it often take a long time for breakthroughs to become visible? Remember, even though the enemy is defeated, he is still intentionally resisting our calls to see God's kingdom come. Even when we long to see God's presence made manifest in our lives, even when we find ourselves praying in alignment with God's Word and will, we can still find our prayers being contested.[6] In these times, we need to keep on believing, trusting, and praying because persistence often breaks resistance. We must not give up as we never know when our miracle may come, and we can be reassured that whilst we are praying, so is he. As Paul says in Romans 8:34: "Christ Jesus who died - more than that, who was raised to life - is at the right hand of God and is also interceding for us." We fight, yes, but we don't fight alone. There are even times when God fights for us!

When God works on the earth, he often uses human agents. We're part of the army of the Lord contending for his Kingdom of light, love, and life to come in areas where principalities and powers bring darkness, destruction, and wickedness. God tells us to fight our battles with spiritual weapons - through praise, prayer, proclaiming God's Word, and persevering faith. So, be encouraged. As you wield these weapons, you wage warfare not in your own human strength but in the mighty power of God's magnificent love that fights with and for us.

As a kid I used to enjoy singing the song, "We want to see Jesus lifted high." I loved the line about every prayer being a powerful weapon, and that when we pray, demonic strongholds come tumbling down. It went down a storm at the kid's holiday club I used to go to as we sang and performed all the actions. The truth is, when we fight God's way, we fight *from* victory not *for* it. We fight an already defeated foe. What we're doing is enforcing the already achieved victory of Christ in every area. That's when strongholds tumble!

WHEN THE FLAMES ROAR

As we enter the dark times where God's plans can feel like a complete mystery, what we need most are reassuring signs that he is present with us in our suffering, making a way through raging fires and roaring seas. I'm going to finish this chapter with an example of how God shows up in both these kinds of contexts.

First, let's look at raging fires. Remember Hananiah, Meshaal, and Azariah? They're more commonly known by their Babylonian-given names - Shadrach, Meshach, and Abednego. These boys were friends of Daniel, a Jewish prophet in exile with them in the pagan and ungodly nation of Babylon.

When the king of that nation – a man called Nebuchadnezzar – commanded everyone in his kingdom to bow down to an enormous golden statue that his craftsmen had made, these three boys said no. They were commanded by God not to worship idols and carved images. They chose obedience to the King of Heaven above obedience to an earthly king.

These boys were brought before King Nebuchadnezzar who flew into a rage. He told them that if they continued to refuse to obey his orders, he would have them thrown alive into a blazing furnace. "Who is the god who will deliver you?" he asks. Their answer is truly profound. This is what they say in Daniel 3:17-18:

"Our God whom we serve is able to deliver us from the burning fiery furnace, and he will deliver us from your hand, O king. But if not, let it be known to you, O king, that we do not serve your gods, nor will we worship the gold image which you have set up."

Look at their words. "Our God is able to deliver us." In other words, our God can do miracles. Then they add, "But if he does not..." This is their recognition of mystery. Sometimes, God doesn't show up in the way we expect or want.

This is precisely the road we travel as Christians. God can do miracles and sometimes does. "Our God is able." He does miracles. But at other times, God chooses to let us walk through the fire rather than be lifted from it. When this happens, he walks with us into the furnace. He gives hints of his presence. He is with us in our adversity, near to us in the mystery. He is our shepherd, tapping on the rocks.

So, what happens? In Daniel 3, the three boys are indeed thrown into a furnace that this cruel king has made seven times hotter than it normally is. But when they do, they find that they are not alone, and the king is the first to notice it (verses 24-25).

King Nebuchadnezzar was astonished; and he rose in haste and spoke, saying to his counsellors, "Did we not cast three men bound into the midst of the fire?"
They answered and said to the king, "True, O king."
"Look!" he answered, "I see four men loose, walking in the midst of the fire; and they are not hurt, and the form of the fourth is like the Son of God."

There is a fourth man in the furnace. One like the Son of God. One who truly was the Son of God. The Second Person of the Trinity. Why is he there? Because God promises his children that when we pass through the fire, he walks with us too. His presence is with us.

These three boys have a truly remarkable faith. We might call it an integrated or holistic faith. They do not believe that God is either a Miracle Worker or a Way Maker. They believe he is both. And when they pass through the fire, God shows up as both, which is why they aren't even singed by the flames.

And what does the king make of all this? He cries "Blessed be the God of Shadrach, Meshach, and Abed-Nego, who sent his Angel and delivered his servants who trusted in him!" (verse 28).

WHEN THE OCEANS ROAR

We see this again in the story I have already mentioned in this chapter – Jesus stilling the storm. In Mark chapter 4, we find Jesus on the shore with his disciples. He tells them that it's time to cross the Sea of Galilee. Leaving the crowds behind, Jesus settles down in the stern of the boat while the disciples set sail and start steering a course across the sea. All goes well at first. But then, as often happens in this part of the world, a storm suddenly appears from nowhere. This is so intense that even the experienced seafarers among them are concerned, especially when water begins to fill the boat. As their concern turns to outright terror, they turn to Jesus.

This is what Mark reports in verse 38:
He was in the stern, asleep on a pillow. And they awoke him and said to him, 'Teacher, do you not care that we are perishing?'

Notice how Mark records that Jesus was asleep "on a pillow". Mark's storytelling is usually not full of small details, but, in this instance, he makes an exception. Mark wants us to notice just how relaxed and comfortable Jesus was. While the wind was howling and the disciples were panicking, Jesus was fast asleep, his head leaning into a cushion that no doubt belonged to the boat owner, Simon Peter. What a picture this is! Jesus can rest and even sleep in the darkness and turbulence of the Sea of Galilee.

How can he do that? Jesus, as God's Son, knows that his heavenly Father is far greater than any storm he might encounter. As a trusting Son, he rests in the revelation that whatever is thrown at him in life, his God is higher, stronger, and mightier. The disciples, on the other hand, don't yet have this level of assurance. Their focus is on the towering waves, the howling wind, and the lashing rain. Consequently, while Jesus lives from a centre of love, they live from a centre of fear. While he rests, they're restless. While he sleeps, they panic.

These are the two kinds of response we have when we pass through the raging waters of life. We can either react from a place of fear or respond from a place of love. The disciples are terrified. Their instinct is to tell God how big the storm is. Jesus is the opposite. His default setting is to tell the storm how big his God is. Jesus recognizes that this storm is sinister and has been sent against him to destroy him. He therefore *rebukes* the storm. The word 'rebuke' is the same Mark elsewhere uses when Jesus is delivering those who are oppressed by demons. He rebukes the storm in the same way that he rebukes the demons.[7]

Look at verses 39-40:
He arose and rebuked the wind, and said to the sea, "Peace, be still!" And the wind ceased and there was a great calm. But He said to them, "Why are you so fearful?"

Jesus doesn't want us to live in fear. He wants us to live in love. He calls us to pull up a pillow and rest in the love of the Father when our minds are confronted by mystery. God Almighty is on board, and we know the promise of Isaiah 43:2:

When you pass through the waters,
  I will be with you;
and when you pass through the rivers,
  they will not sweep over you.
When you walk through the fire,
  you will not be burned;
  the flames will not set you ablaze.

THE GIFT-GIVING FATHER

I return at the end of this chapter to where I began, with Jesus's teaching on prayer. He said to his disciples that God is a loving Father who longs to give us his presence. Even earthly dads know how to give good things to their kids. How much more does our perfect Father in Heaven give the Holy Spirit to those who ask him.

As I wrote earlier, it is important to notice that in Luke 11 Jesus refrains from saying "good gifts" and says instead "the Holy Spirit." He refrains from promising us his presents (with a t) and promises instead his presence (with a c).

Whenever we enter times of trial, our natural inclination is to ask God for powerful presents – for gifts like healing and miracles. Maybe we are facing a sudden life-threatening illness (like my mother did), or a more gradual one (like my father-in-law). In such moments, we almost always ask Jesus to reveal himself through healing and miraculous works. And that's okay. But what if God is calling us to walk through the valley rather than around it?

There are times when God wants to deliver us from our

pain (through miracles) and there are times when he wants us to know his presence in our pain (through his way-making). In either case, the one prayer he will always answer is for his presence.

All you need to do is ask.

FOOTNOTES

1. In Luke 11:13, Jesus says "how much more will your Father in heaven give the Holy Spirit to those who ask him." In Matthew 7:11, Jesus says "good gifts" where Luke has "the Holy Spirit."

2. *Footprints* (sometimes also known as *Footprints in the Sand*) is a poem of unknown authorship. At least twelve people in recent years have claimed that they wrote it! Some of the content may go back to the 19th century. The text is as follows:

One night I dreamed a dream.
As I was walking along the beach with my Lord.
Across the dark sky flashed scenes from my life.
For each scene, I noticed two sets of footprints in the sand,
One belonging to me and one to my Lord.

After the last scene of my life flashed before me,
I looked back at the footprints in the sand.
I noticed that at many times along the path of my life,
especially at the very lowest and saddest times,
there was only one set of footprints.

This really troubled me, so I asked the Lord about it.
"Lord, you said once I decided to follow you,
You'd walk with me all the way.
But I noticed that during the saddest and most troublesome times of my life, there was only one set of footprints.

I don't understand why, when I needed You the most,
You would leave me."
He whispered, "My precious child, I love you
and will never leave you
Never, ever, during your trials and testings.
When you saw only one set of footprints,
It was then that I carried you."

3. Pete Greig speaks about the rarity of miracles in *God on Mute: Engaging the Silence of Unanswered Prayer*, pp.67ff.

4. Andy Mineo, song entitled, Clarity. Lyrics: https://genius.com/Andy-mineo-clarity-lyrics

5. In John chapters 14-16, Jesus promises his followers the Comforter or Helper. The original Greek word behind this title is *parakletos*. This is a combination of *kletos* (meaning "called") and *para* (meaning "alongside"). *Parakletos* is legal terminology. The *parakletos* in an ancient lawcourt was the person tasked to come alongside you as your defender if you were on trial. Jesus is here referring to the Holy Spirit. We are empowered to give a good testimony by the Holy Spirit, who gives us the wisdom to know what to say.

6. Pete Greig, *God on Mute: Engaging the Silence of Unanswered Prayer*, p.170.

7. We see in Matthew, Mark, and Luke's account of this story that after the winds and waves calm, Jesus and his disciples

land on the shore of the Gadarenes. They immediately meet a demon-possessed man who is one of the most harassed people Jesus encountered. This indicates why the disciples of Jesus encountered difficulties on the way. It's highly likely that the Devil sent the storm to stop Jesus reaching this man. We know Satan works in ways like this, where he opposes an upcoming and imminent breakthrough. He did this before Moses and Jesus were born (when edicts were issued to kill Hebrew boys) and before Jesus launched his ministry (when the Devil showed up to try and tempt him away from his mission). The fact that Jesus *rebukes* this storm indicates that it was demonic and intended to prevent Jesus from performing a miracle of deliverance. We know from the story of Job in the Old Testament that the Devil seeks to wreak havoc in the lives of those faithful to God. When we are living between our prayers and God's answer – when oftentimes the waiting involves turbulence, as it did here in Mark chapter 4 – we need to hear Jesus's words, "Peace! Be still!"

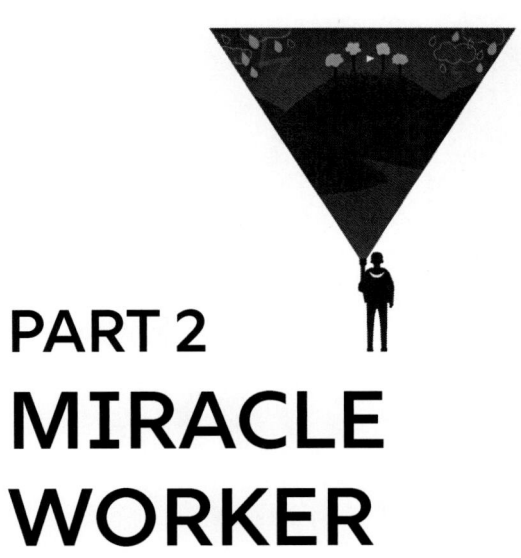

PART 2
MIRACLE WORKER

CHAPTER 4

BATTLES AND BREAKTHROUGHS (JOSH)

One of the greatest miracles Jesus performed is described in John chapter 11. It involved a man called Lazarus, a close friend of Jesus. At the start of the story, there's a verse that feels as if it shouldn't be there. In verse 2, the author talks about Lazarus's sister, Mary, and says this: "It was that Mary who anointed the Lord with fragrant oil and wiped His feet with her hair, whose brother Lazarus was sick."[1] Why does John remind us that this Mary was the one who expressed such devotion to Jesus? One reason is to help the reader identify which Mary he's talking about here – Lazarus's sister. I also believe it's because God wants to teach us something, and that's this: *however deep and real our worship of Jesus may be, we're not going to be immune from troubling and testing times.* Pouring the oil of worship on the feet of Jesus does not inoculate us against suffering.

Here's an example. Both my parents were serving and worshipping Jesus during the season when I was far from God.

My dad was a pastor, and my mum led a prayer movement. They were seeing lives changed and witnessing miraculous answers to prayer, all this while they were suffering because of my rebellion and having to pray for their own son to make it home alive. Often, I was out getting drunk with my friends. Sometimes I'd wake up not knowing where I was.

Before we dive deeper into my story, it's important to say that just because you're going through a tough season, that doesn't mean you're a bad mother, father, brother, sister, grandparent, whatever. You can be like *that* Mary - a radical worshipper and follower of Jesus - yet facing great challenges as she was. When you do, you need to know that God is listening to your pain just as attentively as he is to your praise. God is listening to your heartfelt groans and cries, and he is a specialist in making a way where there seems to be no way. He helps us through our difficulties, as we read in the last chapter. No matter how strange it may feel, it's his way that he's making.

Even when God intervenes dramatically, this can happen during circumstances that don't seem to make sense. God parted the Red Sea and set his people free, yes, but the years of agony and slavery before this would have seemed mystifying to the Israelites. Even miracles are not without mystery! What we need to guard against is allowing this sense of mystery to make us inactive. Let's not allow the pain and disappointment we feel to paralyse us into a state of prayerlessness. Let's rise and contend for God's will to be done. Let's hold on to the belief that miracles still *can* and still *do* happen, as you'll read about in this section of the book. I'll explore this a bit more in a moment but for now it's crucial for us to remember that our prayers matter to our powerful and loving Heavenly Father, and they are heard by him too.

Before we celebrate God as our Miracle Worker, we therefore need to make sure we don't miss the miraculous dimension to God's more gradual way-making. We can often define miracles in a very narrow sense, restricting them to instant healings and other examples of immediate divine intervention. God does indeed act in these ways as you'll read in the pages that follow, but what if, even when he is making a way where there seems to be no way, he is also performing miracles? What if, during painful years of trouble, there are shifts taking place in which God forms things like resilience, faith for the impossible, and persistent prayer in us? As an imperfect person who can be rather stubborn and unwilling to change, I regard these inner changes as miracles. In these arduous times, we're called to stand our ground and trust in the Way Maker God for whom the word 'impossible' is not part of his vocabulary.

LOVE PRAYS DIFFERENT

On Friday 19th May 1989, I was born at Wythenshawe Hospital, Manchester, UK. Today, having three kids of my own, I can imagine the joy my parents felt. I don't think for one moment they anticipated what would unfold over the next eighteen years but before we come to that I want to highlight the moment of my birth. Why? Because on that day, my parents' love for me was born and, as one of the founding pastors of our church - Karen Wheaton – says (in her endearing Alabaman accent), "Love prays different!"[2] What does she mean by that?

In the Garden of Gethsemane, Jesus prayed to his heavenly Father, "not my will but yours be done." This expressed his radical willingness to obey God's will even to the point of dying on the cross.

How was he able to pray such a bold prayer?

The answer? Love!

It was his great love for us that drove Jesus to the cross and it was that love which gave him the strength to pray such a difficult prayer. Hebrews 12:2 says, "for the joy set before him he endured the Cross." You and I were the joyful outcome Jesus had in mind while he was suffering the agony of his crucifixion. That's what we need to fix our eyes on too. This is the key to endurance and perseverance when we are going through pain. We need to love that wayward child, sick family member, broken spouse, or difficult colleague. It is love that strengthens our prayers, fortifies our faith, and deepens our resolve.

In Luke 11 the disciples ask Jesus to teach them how to pray. As part of his response, Jesus tells them a story.

"Which of you shall have a friend, and go to him at midnight and say to him, 'Friend, lend me three loaves; for a friend of mine has come to me on his journey, and I have nothing to set before him'; and he will answer from within and say, 'Do not trouble me; the door is now shut, and my children are with me in bed; I cannot rise and give to you'? I say to you, though he will not rise and give to him because he is his friend, yet because of his persistence he will rise and give him as many as he needs." (Luke 11:5-8).

Jesus shows us here how persistence is key when it comes to prayer. Whenever we experience a crisis, we can't just say, "I'm a friend of God. He'll sort it out." We need to go to our friend's house, knock on his door, and call out, "Hey friend, I need your help!" This may require persistent knocking until the door is opened, the request is answered, and the crisis resolved. In my parents' case, the crisis was their son's waywardness. Their response was to go on knocking on God's door for years. During that season, there were many twists and turns. But God was working all things together through a love that prayed differently.

Love keeps us praying when we run out of words and energy.
Love elevates our faith and hope that God can move.
Love is what we hold on to when all seems lost.
Love carries us along the way that God is making until the moment we see the miracle.

SIX YEARS OF WANDERING

There were times when I did go to church during my wayward years, but I found myself preferring the fun, the social activities to the serious ones. These provided a distraction to activities like prayer and worship. Don't get me wrong, the fun stuff is beneficial, but when the statistics tell us most people start following Jesus before the age of 18, I should have been prioritising the spiritual over the social. That said, despite my lack of spiritual engagement, my parents and youth leaders never stopped loving me and didn't ever give up praying.

As things deteriorated at school I started to question my

life. At some of my lowest moments, I harboured thoughts of suicide. I was desperate to be accepted by people at my school, and this caused me to feel like I had to turn into a different person and put on a front. At times I found myself becoming angry, cold, and aggressive. I often presented that I was okay, but I was broken inside. I turned to everything and anything in life that provided mood-altering pleasure and masked the inner turmoil I was suffering.

When I came to the end of my time in high school, not one of my close friends was a Christian and I had no desire to follow Jesus or go to church anymore. I continued the partying lifestyle and lived life the way I wanted. I experienced major highs but much worse lows which I tried to hide from my parents. All along they were praying for me, along with an army of intercessors. As I approached my eighteenth birthday, things became about as bad as they could. I always say I think I turned my dad grey. All my pictures of him when I was little show him with brown hair. He's grey in the ones when I'm a teenager. We laugh about it now but there is no denying the pain a parent feels when they see their child - someone they love more than anything in the world - wasting and wrecking their life.

It was between the ages of 12 and 18 that I was at my worst. I'm sure many of you reading this have had to battle a lot longer than six years. You may still be battling. It can be very difficult to know what or how to pray in tiring times like these. Church and conference meetings you once loved can end up reinforcing the fact that your prayers haven't been answered, leaving you cynical and frustrated. Although stories of breakthrough can cause many to give God praise, they can also deepen some people's bitterness and anger towards God. It's so important in these times not to distance yourself from God or from your community. Don't allow the enemy to isolate you. Sometimes the easiest thing is to run away, but these are the times we need Jesus and his church the most. God gave us his presence and his people to prevent us facing these battles alone. And let's not forget that Jesus is in heaven right now continually praying for us.

BOWL-TIPPING POINTS

So often it is at the darkest hour, when all hope seems lost, that God begins to break into our lives. May 2007 was that moment for me. I was at the lowest point in my life, locked up in a cold holding-cell in a police station. I was due to stay there from Friday night until my appearance in court the following Monday morning. I don't mind admitting that I was worried about what Monday would bring. I had smashed a load of shop windows with a mate in the local town centre and the police wanted to teach me a lesson by locking me up for an entire weekend, or so it seemed to me. Those days felt like an eternity. I had plenty of time to ponder how my life had descended into such a mess. As I did, it dawned on me that the rot set in when I stopped going to church. I remembered how Mum would often pray for me every night before I went to sleep. Before she prayed for me, she would ask, "Is there anything you're worried or troubled about?"

As I lay on my bed in the cell, I knew there was a lot about my life that gave me cause to be anxious, but I also realised that I had never prayed about these things. There and then, I decided to pray. Falling to my knees I said, "God ... if you're there ... if you're real ... if you care ... please help me... I'm a mess."

As I prayed, something shifted.

Pete Greig says, "God has two speeds - slow and suddenly."[3] There had been tiny cracks in the wall over a long period. As my parents and others had prayed for me, God had moved slowly but surely in my life, preparing me for this moment of breakthrough. As I prayed in my cell, God's slowly turned into a suddenly. God is so mighty that he does both, and so much more. The 'suddenly' moments are often the culmination of the prayers and tears that have built up over time until a tipping point occurs. In Revelation 5:8 and 8:3-5, we see a beautiful picture of what goes on in the spirit realm during these slow seasons. They portray angels, over time, collecting our prayers in bowls. When the bowls are full, they tip and the effects of all these prayers are poured out on the earth with mighty results. In that police station, I was about to be the beneficiary of one of these bowl-tipping points.

After I had prayed for the first time in years, I was overwhelmed by what I now know as the presence of God. I had never felt anything like it. At the same time, it wasn't just a feeling. Sometimes words seem so inadequate when describing encounters like this. What I was experiencing transcended every high I had ever had. It was far greater than intoxication, far better than gratification, far more powerful than any altered state of consciousness I had ever entered. It was like my own personal Day of Pentecost. Maybe you remember the original version, when God suddenly poured out his Spirit. The disciples were so surprised by joy that people thought they were drunk!

James Aladiran says, "When I preach, I can move men and women. But when I pray, I can move angels and demons."[4] My parents' prayers had created a bowl-tipping moment in which demons departed, and angels arrived. What I didn't realise until later was that Mum was praying at the same moment. If only we could see what is going on in the spirit-world as we pray. There I was in a police cell, a blubbering wreck as God blew my mind, softened my heart, and broke into my world with his personal and powerful presence.

MY MOTHER'S SONG

As I was crying, I had a strange experience. I began to hear my mum singing a song I used to sing in church as kid. "And I will rise on eagle's wings." It was audible. I honestly thought that Mum had come to the police station and was singing somewhere nearby. Mum is one of those fearless (and slightly embarrassing) people who really doesn't care what anyone thinks about her. You'll therefore understand why I assumed she was literally in the police station.

I stood, ready for a police officer to let her in to see me. But then the singing began to fade.

I started to feel a rising panic. Maybe the police had turned her away because they wanted to teach me a lasting lesson. That's when I prayed a prayer that you should never pray unless you mean it (which I'm not sure I did). You know the one. "God if you get me out of this situation, I'll live for you forever."

That's a dangerous thing to say to the omnipresent God! God hears our words, and he sees our hearts. The good news is that even when our prayers are flawed, God can somehow still work with them. That's not an excuse to live however we want and still expect God to bless us. It's a realisation that he can do a lot with a little. He takes even our messed-up prayers very seriously.

I arrived in court on Monday morning. For no good reason, the judge seemed to want to be as lenient as possible with me. Even though I was ordered to wear an electronic tag, he tempered justice with mercy. Reminds me of someone else I know! In other words, God made a way for me where there was no way.

This way-making had been building up for some time. Even when it doesn't look the way we want it to, God is still working. Now, when I experienced his amazing presence in that police station, my miracle had come. That miracle not only changed my inner world. It also transformed my outward circumstances. I was free to go. Dad picked me up in the car outside the court. He looked shocked when he saw me. "You seem different," he said.

That was another sign for me – a sign that God was real – *is* real – and that he had been making a way and working a miracle in my life. But it wasn't the biggest sign. That happened when I got home and started sharing my experience with Mum.

"Thanks for coming to the police station and singing for me there," I said.

Mum looked confused. "What do you mean?"

"I heard you singing Eagle's Wings."

"But I never came to the police station."

It was my turn to look confused.

"I was here at home," she said. "Sarah and I were praying all night that you would encounter Jesus." (Sarah is my sister).

Then came the words that turned my world upside down.

"We sang Eagle's Wings here while we were praying. You must have heard it eight miles away! We sang it as a prophetic declaration to call you home."

I could feel my heart melting.

Mum cried, "Josh! This is a miracle!"

It truly was. I still weep when I think about it. God had been hard at work making a way when there seemed to be no way. Even when we couldn't see it, he was making a way. Then, when the bowl tipped, heaven invaded my cell, displacing the hell I had brought upon myself. In other words, he intervened in a dramatic and marvellous way. His slowly turned into a suddenly.

LORD AS WELL AS SAVIOUR

For the next few months, I walked around in shock at how real God is. At the same time, I didn't want to change my sinful life. I was eighteen at the time, and I had friends who enjoyed partying. This meant that I lived in a conflicted state, trying to love the Father while loving the world. There were many nights when I'd cry as I went to sleep.

This highlights something important. Whenever we

experience a breakthrough, we need to remember that God is our Way Maker not just our Miracle Worker. Miracles are instantaneous and immediate, but way-making consists of a long journey in which we need to grow in maturity and walk closer to Jesus as disciples. If miracles involve a crisis, way-making involves a process. The miracle leads to us giving a high-five of praise. The way-making involves us walking hand in hand with Jesus on a long walk of transformation.

In the Bible, we often see how the enemy likes to come in and destroy things in their infancy. When Moses the deliverer was born, Pharaoh tried to kill him by slaughtering the baby boys born to his Hebrew slaves. Likewise, when Jesus was born, Herod the King engaged in a slaughter of the innocents. After my encounter with Jesus, it seemed like the opportunities to go out partying and to fall into sin went into overdrive. At the same time, I could never get away from the fact that I had truly met with God.

In September 2007, some three months after the police station encounter, I found myself at the Message Trust in Manchester where I heard the evangelist Andy Hawthorne preach the Gospel. One of the points he made stuck out for me.

"Jesus can't just be your Saviour," he said. "He must also be your Lord."

Jesus had shown himself as Saviour in that police station.

I knew that.

Now I needed to say yes to him being Lord of my life.

For those three months, I had wrestled with one simple thought. "If I don't give my life to Jesus, I'll spend the rest of my life lying to myself because I know God is real." People were still praying me for even after my police-cell encounter. That's why I often felt such conviction when I sinned - something I'd never known. It was time to stop wavering and draw a line in the sand.

When Andy came to the end of his message, he gave an appeal. "If you want to give your life to Jesus, stand up and do it right now."

My heart raced.

I knew this was my time.

I rose to my feet and gave my whole life to Jesus.

I've never looked back since.

It's been a journey, and many people have had to pastor and help me as a disciple of Jesus, but I've never gone back on that decision to follow Jesus, nor have I ever got over that first-time encounter with Jesus in the most unlikely of places. That was a miracle, and I've seen a quite a few miracles since then too – crisis moments where God has intervened in power. All the while, God has been faithfully making a way for me as he guides, grows, and governs my life for his good. That's been a process, but no less powerful too.

MIRACLES STILL HAPPEN

Even with a conversion story like mine, I've sometimes lost sight of God's ability to do signs and wonders. Sometimes I've found myself growing cynical and jaded, almost expecting miracles *not* to happen. My problem isn't lack of faith. It's having *partial* faith in God. It's accepting and believing that

God is a Way Maker but having trouble knowing him as a Miracle Worker. I'm good at believing that Jesus is with me on the boat when the storm comes but not so good at believing Jesus will command the storm to stop. Maybe you're a bit like me. Maybe your faith is so focused on the God who makes a way that you forget he still does miracles. Yes, they're rare, but they still happen.

Why do we find it so difficult to have a strong faith that God will do signs and wonders? I'd like to suggest six reasons.

The first is *fear*.

Caught in a serious storm, the disciples chose fear instead of faith. Fear can often lull our brains into a state forgetfulness. We miss the obvious – that the one who works wonders is on the boat with us. Jesus challenges his companions to believe that he can do what they consider impossible. He is bigger than the storm. God holds every circumstance together in his sovereign power and love, whether he makes a way through the trial or miraculously rescues us out of it. With eyes of faith, we must stare fear in the face and chose to keep our eyes on Jesus as he calls us out onto the waters of so-called impossibility.

The second is *failure*.

I am guessing a lot of us have thought that God won't do a miracle because we've blown it at some point. While grace isn't a license to continue in sin, the truth is every person in the Bible (except for Jesus), and every Christian that has ever lived, regularly falls short of God's standard. This is not an excuse to lower the bar, but we can't ignore God's amazing grace – that he acts on our behalf, even when we don't deserve it. He delights in showing us mercy. God can and does do miracles even through and for broken people. We must remember that, despite our shortcomings, God can redeem and restore us to believe that greater things can happen.

The third is *frustration*.

The Church is full of broken people (including me and you), which means we often fail one another. When that happens, people can become frustrated with the Church and fall away from their faith. Some say theirs was a "shallow faith" if that happens, but for me that's a harsh and unreasonable thing to say. The Church is called to be the unblemished Bride of Christ, so it's not surprising if some become disillusioned when God's people bruise and abuse each other. Jesus said in John 13:35 that the world would know we're his disciples by our love for another, so it's not wrong to state that the opposite can also be true, that people won't know Jesus due to our lack of love. While we should call people to account for obvious wrongdoing and challenge each other with kindness and conviction for lesser things, we're also called to have grace for one another's regular faults, demonstrating forgiveness and restoration. We're called to justice and mercy because we all fall short of God's high standards. When we do this, we catch a glimpse of the God who forgives, restores, and does miracles. If it wasn't for his restoring love, the stories of many Bible heroes wouldn't have been told.

The fourth is *fallenness*.

In the beginning, God created a perfect world in which Adam and Eve could live. He told them that they would continue to live a perfect life in his presence just so long as they did not eat any fruit from the tree of knowledge. They disobeyed. Consequently, human beings fell from this idyllic state into an imperfect life – one blighted by sin, sickness, suffering, and death. Today, we see evidence of the fallen nature of our world all the time. News of terrible traumas floods our small and big screens like an unstoppable torrent. This turns us into consumers of catastrophe in which we become far more aware of the signs of the fall than we are signs of the Kingdom of Heaven. This subconsciously erodes our faith to the point where, even though we may hope for a positive outcome, we expect a negative one.

The fifth is *fatigue*.

Have you ever prayed for a miracle, and it didn't happen?

Did you pray and pray, and the heavens were like brass?

Did you then become weary?

Did hope deferred make your heart grow sick?

There's no escaping the fact that our prayers sometimes go unanswered. You may be reading this book because you're longing for God to do a miracle. Yet, while you're just about holding on to your belief in God as a Way Maker, you're feeling too fatigued from the fight to believe that he could still show up in your life as a Miracle Worker. We all experience times when we're just too tired to believe that God is going to answer our prayers. Our heads tell us God can still do a miracle, but our hearts have become so weary we struggle to pray for God to intervene. The words of Andy Hawthorne have always inspired me to keep on praying in times like these: "The less I pray, the less miracles I see, but the more I pray, the more miracles seem to happen."[4] Lord, heal our hearts to believe you can still do miracles.

The sixth is *faithlessness*.

Jesus often challenged the disciples about their lack of faith. So, while God can work with mustard-seed faith, he also calls us to increase our belief in him and not settle for little faith. With this in mind, we need to remember that faith is a spectrum. At the strong end, you believe wholeheartedly that which you don't yet see – let's say, that a healing miracle is going to happen. In the middle of the spectrum, there's a measure of doubt. You believe that you may see a breakthrough, but you also believe that you may not. At the lower end of the spectrum, you don't believe at all. This may be because you take the view that miracles happened in Bible times, but not today. Or you may have believed in or even seen miracles before, but you've encountered unanswered prayer or delays, so now you struggle to believe God will or can do them. If you're at the "little faith" end of the spectrum, remember that the habit of questioning things is not in itself wrong. There is without doubt a healthy aspect to it. But when we start questioning everything – including God's power to do miracles – it can become unhealthy. Remember, "faith is confidence in what we hope for and assurance about what we do not see." (Hebrews 11:1). We see it when we believe it.

BACK TO BETHANY

I began this chapter by mentioning Mary, the sister of Lazarus. She is introduced as *that* Mary. *That* Mary was a radical worshipper of Jesus. Jesus would often come to her house because her brother Lazarus was a much-loved friend of his.

One time, she showed her devotion by humbling herself at Jesus's feet and using expensive perfume to anoint the man she knew as her master as well as her friend. The point I made at the beginning of this chapter was this: you can be a dedicated person of prayer and a passionate worshipper of God and yet still go through tough times. My parents have always been committed to a life of worship, yet they – like *that* Mary – had to go through six hard years of seeing me go off the rails.

Another thing that's revealing about Mary of Bethany's story is that it shows how Jesus both makes a way and performs a miracle. He does his way-making work by doing something that looks at first like it doesn't make sense. When he's told his friend Lazarus is seriously ill, he doesn't travel to Bethany straightaway. Let's look at what John reports at the start of chapter 11:

Now a certain man was sick, Lazarus of Bethany, the town of Mary and her sister Martha. It was that Mary who anointed the Lord with fragrant oil and wiped His feet with her hair, whose brother Lazarus was sick. Therefore the sisters sent to Him, saying, "Lord, behold, he whom You love is sick."

When Jesus heard that, He said, "This sickness is not unto death, but for the glory of God, that the Son of God may be glorified through it."

Now Jesus loved Martha and her sister and Lazarus. So, when He heard that he was sick, He stayed two more days in the place where He was.

Look at the two sentences that end this section. The first

says how much Jesus loved Lazarus and his two sisters. This includes *that* Mary. The second says that when he heard how ill Lazarus was, he stayed where he was for two more days. Don't you think that's odd? Why, if Jesus loves them so, doesn't he respond immediately?

This is something we've all experienced. You could call it the *divine delay*. Sometimes it feels as if God delays his answers to our prayers. When he does, we must suppose there's a reason. And there is. Sometimes, what feels like a setback is in fact a setup. In other words, when God doesn't respond immediately, that doesn't mean he's not working. There's a reason why Lazarus's sisters faced a delay in the answer to their desperate prayer. In the eyes of Jesus's contemporaries, the soul left a dead person's body on the fourth day. This is why he delayed until Lazarus had been dead for four days. Jesus wanted to raise Lazarus when people knew it couldn't happen. That way, the miracle would manifest his divine glory. Let's look at how God's way-making transitions into miracle working.

Jesus lifted His eyes and said, "Father, I thank You that You have heard Me. And I know that You always hear Me, but because of the people who are standing by I said this, that they may believe that You sent Me."

Now when He had said these things, He cried with a loud voice, "Lazarus, come forth!"

And he who had died came out bound hand and foot with graveclothes, and his face was wrapped with a cloth.

Jesus said to them, "Loose him, and let him go."

When God doesn't answer straightaway, or in the manner we expect, it might just be because he is building a road in the landscape of impossibility. That takes time, but a moment comes when the miracle can happen, when Jesus stands outside the tomb of his friend and shouts, "Lazarus, come out!" As someone once said, it's a good job he mentioned Lazarus by name. Had he not, there would have been many people walking out of tombs that day! That's how all-powerful God is. When he acts, he makes the impossible possible.

There are many reasons why we don't always see a miracle straightaway when we pray. One of these is because God sometimes chooses to move slowly. That said, it's important that we don't restrict God to moving slowly. He isn't just the God who makes a way through our trials. He is also the one who can perform instantaneous miracles like making the sun stand still or part the oceans. As *that* Mary's story reminds us, he not only moves gradually; he also acts suddenly by waiting until the moment when all seems impossible. That way, he gets the glory, and him alone.

FOOTNOTES

1. This is the NKJV (New King James Version) of verse 2 of John 11: "It was *that* Mary who anointed the Lord with fragrant oil and wiped His feet with her hair, whose brother Lazarus was sick." In the original language, the word "that" conveys the sense of "you know, the Mary who anointed Jesus…"

2. Karen Wheaton, https://www.youtube.com/watch?v=Cq0EJ5L-Cws

3. Pete Greig says this here: https://www.youtube.com/watch?v=PpHa3ww8GB0

4. James Aladiran says this here: https://www.youtube.com/watch?v=_BKaIFTjYW4

5. Although I have no direct sourced for this quotation, I have heard Andy Hawthorne say this while preaching.

CHAPTER 5

THERE CAN BE MIRACLES (DEBRA)

I'm so thankful that I've sometimes seen God do amazing miracles. Take the time we outgrew our office. For ten years we had been occupying a space at the Message Trust headquarters in Sharston, Manchester. This open-plan office had begun to feel smaller than ever. One day, I was having a bit of a grumble about it when the phone rang. It was the Cabinet Office in London. Somehow the government heard we were looking for a new headquarters.

"The Department for Education has an empty building in Partington, not far from the Trafford Centre. It might be available. Are you interested in having a look?"

My heart leapt, and before I could think of a measured response, I had agreed a date and time.

A little bit of research revealed that the building in question was a purpose-built, state-of-the-art community centre that had cost £5.5 million. Constructed in 2011, it had been run by a small, local charity for a year or so but had closed due to lack of funds.

It didn't take Frank long to do some ball-park calculations. "Overheads will be roughly £100,000 per annum. On top of that, we'll need a caretaker, cleaning staff, a receptionist, and maybe more staff, unless we can persuade our current team to add some new tasks to their existing roles."

One thought crossed my mind. *Where are we going to get the money for all that?*

Frank was adamant. "We shouldn't even be considering this. If you go, you'll have to go on your own."

When I arrived in December 2013, the first thing I noticed was the large logo on the outside of the glass-fronted building. The FUSE, painted in four strong colours - the same colours as our ROC logo. That was spinetingling!

I drove into the large car park and noted plenty of outdoor space, including a floodlit 3G five-a-side soccer pitch. Next door there was a secondary school. One of the school staff had the keys to the building. When we entered the main reception area, my eyes were drawn to the 30-foot-high ceiling which made the space seem vast and airy. It was furnished like a large café. The four ROC colours were repeated in the decor and in the signs pointing to the Auditorium, Dance Studio, Sports Hall, Green Room, Art Workshop, Conference Room, and Kitchen. Upstairs there were fully furnished offices with computers, copiers and cupboards. Everything looked brand new. Each room had a large, quirky clock fixed to the wall, made up of individual numbers set in an avant-garde non-circle. You can guess the colours of the numbers!

Even though it had been closed for a year it was in amazing

condition. There was a 300-seat theatre with electrically operated lighting hoists, fully equipped sound system, and enormous cinema screen. The retractable bank of fold-down cinema seats made it ideal for a conference or church meeting.

I was in a bit of a daze, but I knew this was God's new home for us. It ticked every box, but could we make it happen? We would need to put together a business plan to show how we could pay the bills. Would the government give it to us when other groups had been turned away? We would need the favour of God, that's for sure.

Negotiations took six to seven months, during which our prayers moved up a gear as we addressed each of the practical challenges. We appealed to our faithful supporters for a £50,000 fighting fund to enable us to cover costs during our setting-up phase. We set a date by which we needed this before we would sign the lease. One week before the date, the fund hit £60,000.

Hallelujah!

Then came the miracle.

We were offered the building on a 22-year rent-free lease.

I had to pinch myself.

Although there were other questions still to be answered, we knew it was right to say yes.

We signed the lease.

On 29 July 2014 we moved into The FUSE - our amazing and miraculous provision. Everyone agreed that it felt like we were experiencing the unprecedented favour of God!

Over the last ten years, God has continued to help us pay the bills. We have therefore seen two miracles – the provision of the space and the provision of the means to stay.

We experienced another miracle after moving into the new building, something that was so much more than we could have hoped. Our good friend Jon Hancock who worked for the BBC pitched the idea of filming the CBeebies children's TV show from The FUSE. To his amazement, the BBC said yes. That's how we became a filming location! Lots of TV shows have subsequently been filmed there.

Then there was another miracle. We soon found ourselves needing extra staff, but we didn't have a budget for that. This need was unexpectedly met too. The local housing association said they wanted to provide a work placement for a young Romanian woman so that she could learn English. They covered her salary for two years and we gained a receptionist and administrator.

We also discovered how when one door closes another one opens. Salford City Football Club under 18's had been with us for two years and this was helping us to cover the cost of our utilities which are very expensive. They announced they were moving on to a base nearer Salford. Just as they were moving out, a South African Christian called Victoria approached us to ask if she could base her Global make-up Academy with us. They offer make-up and hairdressing lessens for girls to help them into employment. It was a perfect fit!

At around the same time, Carl – a local businessman - approached us to ask if we could convert our basketball court into a padel tennis court. Not only is this amazing news for Partington, but a great new partner for us. Another miracle!

I love the saying, 'provision follows vision'.

Never limit God.
If he opens a door, he will provide.
He doesn't just make a way.
He performs wonders!

DIVINE CREATIVITY

This book is partly inspired by Isaiah 43. I love this passage and it's worth unpacking it a bit more here. In Isaiah 43:14-21, the prophet makes a declaration about God's miraculous provision:

This is what the LORD says - your Redeemer, the Holy One of Israel: "For your sake I will send to Babylon and bring down as fugitives all the Babylonians, in the ships in which they took pride. I am the LORD, your Holy One, Israel's Creator, your King."

This is what the LORD says - he who made a way through the sea, a path through the mighty waters, who drew out the chariots and horses, the army and reinforcements together, and they lay there, never to rise again, extinguished, snuffed out like a wick: "Forget the former things; do not dwell on the past. See, I am doing a new thing! Now it springs up; do you not perceive it? I am making a way in the desert and streams in the wasteland. The wild animals honour me, the jackals and the owls, because I provide water in the desert and streams in the wasteland, to give drink to my people, my chosen, the people I formed for myself that they may proclaim my praise."

When the prophet Isaiah was inspired to speak these words to the people of Israel they were in exile in Babylon. It had been 70 years since Jerusalem had been turned to rubble by the Babylonian army. 50,000 Israelite prisoners were taken to Babylon. The prophet now speaks to them about forgetting the old days and embracing God's new beginnings. The Israelites respond to this challenge in quite a predictable way. Some, gripped by nostalgia, dream of a return to Jerusalem. They sing a song made famous by Bob Marley and Boney M: "By the rivers of Babylon, where we sat down and there we wept when we remembered Zion" (quoting from Psalm 137). This is their cry as they disobey Isaiah's call and longed for their former glory days.

The problem with these folks is they are not able to forget the past. They dream of a restored city and Temple. They want to make Israel great again, as in the days of David and Solomon.

When Isaiah prophesies here, he reminds his original listeners of two miracles to do with water. In the first, God dried up the sea to create a safe passage for the Hebrew slaves as they fled from Pharaoh's chariots. In the second, God provided water in a parched place to alleviate his people's thirst. In the first, God caused the water to dry up, and in the second he caused water to spring up. God responded to the needs of his people in different ways. Parting the sea speaks of God making a way for us where there is no way. Springs in the desert speaks of his miraculous provision when we have no resources left.

The prophet calls the people to do two things - to remember and to forget. These are seemingly contradictory, but they are both important. They needed to remember what God did in the past. The prophet describes the God who performed these miracles: "He who made a way through the sea, a path through the mighty waters, who drew out the chariots and horses, the army and reinforcements together, and they lay there, never to rise again, extinguished, snuffed out like a wick." You will recognise the story. It's the Exodus.

In Exodus 14, we see Pharaoh changing his mind about letting his slaves leave Egypt. As the Hebrews depart, he orders his men to bring them back. The story comes to a climax when Moses and the people stand stranded between the Egyptian army and the raging waves of the Red Sea. There is no way forward and no way back.

In obedience to God's command, Moses stretches out his hand and the waters divide, allowing his followers safe passage. The Egyptians follow them but God again commands Moses to stretch out his hand and the sea engulfs the pursuing army.

Scholars estimate that it took about four hours to cross the Red Sea, so the people had to keep believing in God during this transition. This is an abiding lesson for us today. If ever we feel trapped in a situation, it's important to remember that God didn't remove the Red Sea; he parted it. The prophet reminds them of this fact to build faith and trust in what God wants to for them now. He celebrates with them God's amazing creativity. God is Israel's *Creator*. He does new things that people don't anticipate. He makes a way through the desert. He causes springs of water to appear in barren desert landscapes. His miracles of provision are therefore constantly undergoing innovation. No one can rely on the way he did things in former times. This God is highly original in the way he does things. As C.S. Lewis once said, speaking to writers who thought they were doing something new, "originality is the prerogative of God alone."[1]

MIRACULOUS KEYS

There have been other times when I have witnessed God's miracle-working creativity. These have happened during challenges, trials, and calamity. In each case, God has suddenly broken into our lives. I struggle to come up with a human explanation for these events. I am compelled to acknowledge this is God and say "Wow!"

One of these occurrences was in 2013. I had been invited to speak at Queen's Park Baptist Church in Glasgow. On the Saturday there was a city-wide conference called 'Calling the City to Life.' The next day, I was invited to speak at the Sunday morning service.

As was often the case in those days, I travelled with Wendy, my prayer partner and friend. The week before we left for Scotland, Wendy decided we needed to take some keys with us, so she went to a Timpson store and asked if they had any going spare. They said yes and gave her a large bag of assorted, unwanted keys.

At the conference, I shared stories of the city-wide transformation we had experienced in Manchester. It seemed to raise people's faith and levels of expectation. Towards the end, we distributed the keys randomly to the delegates in the meeting. One of these we gave to a lady from Syria who was seeking asylum in Glasgow. She had lost many members of her family and had very few material possessions. The people at Queen's Park Baptist Church welcomed her into their community and invited her along to the conference. On Sunday, she came to church. She brought the random key she had been given on Saturday.

At the end of the service, this lady walked to the front to show us the key. It was silver and had some initials on it, as well as the number 61. The initials read MSBB. In broken English, she said, "Those are my initials! God knows my name. I have been feeling all alone. But he has not forgotten me."

I shook my head in amazement.

"And the number 61..." she continued. "Today you spoke on Isaiah chapter 61. It all makes sense. He wants to bind up my broken heart, to comfort me, to give me his favour, like it says."

I looked at Wendy in shock. She didn't seem at all surprised. To me it seemed overwhelming to witness God's love for a lady in such deep distress. His kindness to her is a memory I cherish.

Six months later, in 2014, we heard of another miracle involving a key. I was with our team launching Redeeming Our Communities in Scotland. We had hired the Royal Concert Hall and some of the friends we had met at Queen's Park Baptist Church (QPBC) offered to volunteer on the team. Around 1500 people gathered from across Scotland at the auditorium. Before the event started in the evening, we had a meal together and QPBC organised the catering. The lady in charge of the team came running across to me.

"I need to tell you about the key you gave me at the conference in Glasgow."

"Go on."

"I'm a secondary school teacher. On the Monday after

the weekend, I went into my classroom. There is a resources cupboard, but the key to it was lost. There was only one thing for it."

I was all ears.

"I told the class I had been given a key in church that weekend. I told them that I believed the key would open the cupboard. I took the key out of my purse and the key not only fitted in the lock. It opened the cupboard door, and the class gave a cheer."

I marvelled at the woman's faith; she had told the young people that she believed she knew what would happen before she saw it. That's faith - believing what you cannot yet see.

Those are two extraordinary events that have shaped my life in different ways. Both have taught me something about the awe-inspiring creativity of God when it comes to revealing himself as a Miracle Worker in our lives today.

JESUS IN ME

Josh and I believe that God still does miracles today. These miracles are infinitely varied, from dramatic healings to extraordinary provision. As the prophet Isaiah promises (in chapter 35, verses 5-6):

> *Then will the eyes of the blind be opened*
> *and the ears of the deaf unstopped.*
> *Then will the lame leap like a deer,*
> *and the mute tongue shout for joy.*
> *Water will gush forth in the wilderness*
> *and streams in the desert.*

Why don't we see these things more often? There are many answers to that question, but one of them has to do with lack of faith. Now I know what you're thinking. "She means lack of faith in God." I'm not. I'm referring more to faith in ourselves. Many of us don't have a problem believing that God can do a miracle through someone else – someone holy, charismatic, well-known. But we do have a problem believing that God can do a miracle *through* us. In other words, we are fine about believing in God. We are not so fine about the idea of God believing in us – not enough to do miracles through us.

I remember being on the leadership and speaking team at a Christian conference called Spring Harvest. This takes place at Butlins holiday camp every Easter. Thousands of people gather there from churches across the UK. On the first night, I was walking through an area called the Skyline after the celebration. It was bustling with people looking at the various exhibition stands and meeting up for coffee with friends. I spotted a couple and felt prompted to stop for a conversation. The lady was in a wheelchair and her husband was assisting her.

"Have you been to Spring Harvest before?" I asked.

"It's our second year."

After a bit of small talk, I asked, "Is it okay if you tell me why you're in this wheelchair?"

"I've had polio since I was a child. Despite that, I've had a good life, a wonderful marriage, and had children."

"Are you looking around the exhibition?" I asked.

"No," she replied. "We're looking for Jim. He's a volunteer. We met him here last year. He prayed for me. One of the symptoms of polio is difficulty with breathing. I love to worship and wanted to sing in the meetings. But I was getting breathless. Jim prayed and I was not only able to breathe more easily, but also sing all week."

"Why do you want to see him?"

"I want to ask him to pray for me again."

All I could think of was what if Jim hadn't volunteered (which, as it turned out, he hadn't).

"May I pray for you instead?" I asked.

She nodded.

I prayed for her to have breath in her lungs and for her to be able to sing. She smiled and breathed deeply. I left trusting God that he would answer and that she would have a great week.

I felt elated that night that I was able to be a channel of God's blessing to her. Afterwards, I reflected on this conversation and had this thought so clearly. Everyone is looking for Jim. Everyone needs someone to stand in the gap for them. They're looking for a friendly smile, a prayer, a conversation, a helping hand. But then I became even more excited when I had the thought that JIM is an acronym for 'Jesus in me.' Jesus is in me wanting to reach out to others. I need to make myself available and be willing to be used. So, believe in yourself as well as God. You can do it. You're a Jim. Someone needs you today.

NOW OR NOT YET

If we don't believe in ourselves, if we don't have a proper appreciation of our identity as God's adopted sons and daughters, and the spiritual authority that comes with this precious and privileged identity, then we may miss those opportunities to pray for miracles that come our way - or at least to pray again. Quite often we pray micro-prayers and expect microwave answers. Have we tried persisting in prayer? Or waiting on God? Sometimes the miracle can take longer than expected – as it did for the sisters of Lazarus.

Having said that, we need also to recognise there are mysteries on God's side too. These are to do with the Kingdom of God, sometimes referred to as the Kingdom of Heaven. At the start of the Gospels of Mark, Matthew, and Luke, we see Jesus beginning his public ministry. He cries out to the people that the Kingdom of God has come. What did he mean by that? Jesus was saying that the rule of Satan over this world – a rule resulting in sin, suffering, and death – was coming to an end and that the rule of God – a rule resulting in forgiveness, healing, and life – was beginning. It was beginning in and through Jesus of Nazareth because Jesus is the King of the Kingdom. Jesus, as the Son of God, has the authority to forgive people their sins (through his words) and the power to release people from their oppression by the devil (through his works). In his public ministry, the Kingdom of God enters human history. It is announced through his message (proclamation) and confirmed by his miracles (demonstration).

These miracles are very varied in character. There are, firstly, *healing* miracles. These are sudden demonstrations of kingdom power in which Jesus cures the sick. There are, secondly, *deliverance* miracles. In these, he instantly liberates people from demonic oppression. There are, thirdly, miracles of *provision*. In these, Jesus miraculously supplies the needs of those who are hungry, as he did with the feeding of the 5000.

There are fourthly, *nature* miracles, such as when Jesus stilled the storm on the Sea of Galilee. There are finally the *resurrection* miracles in which Jesus raised dead people, such as Lazarus, back to life. All these miracles were signs that the Kingdom of God had arrived in and through the person of Jesus. God's reign, expected at the end of history, had arrived ahead of time in Jesus's words and works. As Jesus said in Matthew 12:28, "If it is by the Spirit of God that I drive out demons, then the kingdom of God has come upon you."

That last comment is crucial for understanding how miracles are performed by Jesus. It is by 'the Spirit of God' that these things happen. When someone was dramatically healed, this was not by magic (illusion) but by miracles (intervention). When Jesus raised Lazarus, it was because the power of God's Holy Spirit moved in response to his prayer to his Father. Every authentic miracle was performed by the Father, through the Son, and in the power of the Holy Spirit. That's why Jesus could say that the kingdom of God had come when he delivered a demonized person. Every miracle done by Jesus, or in his name, is a sign that the rule of God – Father, Son, and Holy Spirit – has come. This is why miracles are so important. They confirm, attest, and prove that our claim is true when we say, "the Kingdom of God is here!"

Why, then, don't we see miracles *every* time we pray? The answer is because the kingdom of God began to appear on the earth two thousand years ago (at Jesus's first coming) but it won't be fully present all over the earth until sometime in the future (at his second coming). Jesus taught that the Kingdom of God is something that grows, expands, and advances between his first and second coming. The parable of the mustard seed is an example – it begins tiny but grows into a big tree (Mark 4:30-32). God's rule arrived in Jesus's first coming. Between then and his second coming, it grows like a seed and spreads like yeast. The kingdom of God is partly now here in the world and not yet fully here on earth. Quite the paradox! These two aspects of God's kingdom, "now" and "not yet", are crucial for understanding why miracles sometimes don't happen after our most heartfelt prayers. Sometimes God answers by saying, "Now." The kingdom of God comes in power and the sick are healed. But sometimes he says, "Not yet." In other words, the person is not healed now but is promised their healing in the world to come (when the kingdom has been fully established).

MY FRIEND STEVE

What we are talking about here is two different answers to our prayers for healing. The first answer is not yet. This is the valley of mystery. The second answer is now. This is the mountaintop of miracle. It can be very hard sometimes to traverse such varied terrain.

I have learned so much from those who have navigated their way through this challenging landscape. I am thinking right now of my good friends, Steve and Bekah Legg. I have known Steve for about thirty years and worked alongside him at events like Spring Harvest, Festival Manchester, and Thank God for Christmas. Steve was a comedian, magician, author, broadcaster, magazine editor (founder of the brilliant men's magazine called *Sorted*), and speaker. Steve had the ability to make you laugh on and off the platform. He was brilliant at putting on all-age events with his family-friendly style of entertainment. Above all, he was passionate about sharing the Good News and loved seeing people coming to know Jesus.

Frank and I often visited their home in Littlehampton. We also went on retreat with them and others several times in Somerset. It was at one of those retreats in 2021 that Steve's foot was hurting. Anyone who knew Steve, also knew he loved a long walk, often with friends or with his dog Colbie. To see him struggling caught our attention but it didn't seem to be anything too serious. However, following a medical investigation, his doctor said the lump needed to be removed. One thing seemed to lead to another. The diagnosis was not good. Steve tells the whole story in his brilliant book *The Last Laugh*.[2]

On April 17th 2023, Steve was told he only had five months to live. Hundreds of people, including Frank and I, joined a prayer group to ask God for a miracle. Bekah regularly updated us so we could intercede in a focused way. We all prayed for God to heal Steve.

One thing I vividly remember was their decision to have a 'summer of joy' in 2023. They chose joy rather than despair. *If* it was to be their last summer, they would make the most of every second. As it turned out, Steve didn't die in September 2023 as the doctor had estimated. He lived until September 16th 2024.

Just after Easter 2024, Steve organised another one of his famous retreats, this time in Antibes! A very kind lady who had read his book *The Last Laugh* offered him two lovely houses for a week. Ten of us duly set off together to one of the most beautiful places on earth. That week away was the most fun Frank and I had had in years. We laughed until the tears were streaming down our faces. It was such a precious time. It felt to us like a bonus, with Steve having been told he was going to die six months previously.

During the weeks after Steve was told he was going to die, he and Bekah developed a way of dealing with the challenge of living with a life-ending illness in a way that made room for both miracle and mystery. Bekah came to call this "twin-track living". On the one hand, she and Steve remained firmly rooted to a miracle track. They asked God, and continued to ask God, to heal Steve. They asked for the Kingdom of God to come *now*. In a sense, you could say that it did. Steve lived almost exactly a year longer than he was told by the experts. That year was a year of joy. As Steve put it, he got busy living, and he got busy laughing. Those who spent time with him and Bekah during this final phase will never forget how he and they lived life to the full. In other words, God healed him enough to enjoy a year of joy. On the other hand, God did eventually call Steve home. The answer was therefore *not yet*. Steve will be fully healed when he is raised with a new, resurrection body – one that will never need the attentions of a dermatologist or an oncologist again. That is the mystery track.

"Twin-track living" is a perfect description of how we are called to live in a landscape of mystery and miracles. Sometimes we see God slowly making a way for us, walking alongside us in the dark valley of the shadow of death. At other times, we see him doing sudden and dramatic wonders. For Bekah, walking this road of mystery and miracles meant praying for Steve's healing with sincere faith while at the same time making practical preparations for the possibility of his death – organising insurance, hospice care, and so on. This "twin-track" perspective enabled them both to enjoy life. As Bekah said at Steve's thanksgiving service, "He left us wanting more."

Bekah spoke after Steve's death about twin-track living in what she calls "the unshakable kingdom of God". I'll leave the last words of this chapter to her:

"There is something about this unshakable kingdom of God that I have been learning the last couple of years. I have come to know that my faith in God and my joy, my contentment, all those things, they aren't dependent on the world being exactly as I want. So even though the ending wasn't the fairy tale, there have been so many moments when God has just been incredibly gracious and kind to us. I've learned to see that God is doing things all over the place, even if he doesn't answer every single request with a big fat yes in the way that we want. It has been the most wonderful life lesson that so often two things coexist.

You can have sadness, but there's still joy to be found. There can be great times, but there's still pain somewhere in the offering. And I think if you can live life accepting that, not needing everything to be perfect for it to be good, then actually happiness is a lot easier to find."[3]

FOOTNOTES

1. C.S. Lewis, in his essay, 'Christianity and Literature' (1939), pp.7-8. See https://matiane.wordpress.com/2023/12/04/christianity-and-literature-by-c-s-lewis/

2. Steve Legg, *The Last Laugh*. Son Christian Media Ltd. 2024.

3. Bekah Legg's interview is with Mark Dowd. You can find 'The Toughest Christmas' at https://www.thingsunseen.co.uk/podcasts/the-toughest-christmas/

PART 3
PROMISE KEEPER

CHAPTER 6

GOOD NEWS STORIES (DEBRA)

It's been exciting up until now to remember how God makes a way for us when there seems to be no way (Way Maker), and how he performs signs that make us wonder (Miracle Worker). As we've looked at scriptures and stories about both, you may have noticed that these two focus more on individuals rather than communities. Although God's way making and miracle working may touch the lives of a wider group of people, they primarily impact the person walking through dark times, or the person crying out to God for a dramatic intervention. When we come to God as Promise Keeper and Light Bringer, the reach is bigger. These two focus more on communities than individuals. As God fulfils his promises and sheds his light, although individuals may be the starting point, the reach is larger - communities and even nations.

The God of the Bible is truly worthy of being called the Promise Keeper. The Bible contains 8,810 promises, with 7,487 of them promises made by God to humankind. These cover a wide range of things - salvation, comfort, new life, spiritual blessings, peace, meeting people's needs, strength, guidance, rescue and redemption. Having been in pastoral ministry for over forty years I can safely say that I have seen him fulfil these promises both in my life and other people's lives many times. God makes promises because he cares deeply for people. Like the best fathers, our Father in heaven keeps the promises he makes to his sons and daughters – promises such as "I will never leave you nor forsake you" (Hebrews 15:5), "I will repay the years the locusts have eaten" (Joel 2:25). I have shared both these verses with individuals just in the last few days. Such statements are hugely encouraging for anyone going through a difficult time. I often say to myself and others that we need to recite these words over and over. We should write them in our journals, put them on our fridges, underline them in our Bibles, repeat them in our prayers. We should use them to silence the accusations of the enemy as well as the voice of self-doubt.

Remember Jesus when he was tempted in the wilderness, facing hunger and extreme tiredness. He said, "Man shall not live by bread alone but by every word which comes from the mouth of God." Jesus knew the power of the Word of God and was able to apply it when resisting the devil in the desert. God's Word therefore is mighty for fending off the enemy. His promises have the power to sustain you, to transform any situation, and to bring the breakthrough you need. This was true for me when Josh was away from the Lord. It was also true when I had my recent health scare. I looked to what God was saying rather than what circumstances indicated. When I was seriously ill God spoke to me from Psalm 139:7-10:

Where can I flee from your presence? If I go up to the heavens, you are there; if I make my bed in the depths, you are there. If I rise on the wings of the dawn, if I settle on the far side of the sea, even there your hand will guide me, your right hand will hold me fast.

There is more than a hint of promise in these words. See how the simple little word "will" features here. "Even there your hand *will* guide me, your right hand *will* hold me fast." If I fly to 35,000 feet in an airbus, I *will* find God's presence high above the clouds. If I dive in a submersible to the bottom of the ocean, I *will* know that he is with me there as well. The promises of God are so powerful. They keep us hopeful and increase our capacity to persevere.

I WILL POUR OUT MY SPIRIT

While some of God's promises can be applied to individuals, there are many that are intended for communities, societies, nations, and even the world. Look at the most famous promise of revival in Scripture, 2 Chronicles 7:14. God promises that he will forgive people's sins if they humble themselves, pray, turn from their wicked ways, and seek his face. He also promises that he will "heal the land." The Hebrew word translated 'land' is *eretz*. It is used in the phrase 'the Promised Land' and in 'the land of Canaan.' This shows that the impact of people returning to God in repentance is not just individual but communal and even environmental. When God pours out his Spirit in revival, it's not just those praying who encounter the goodness and grace of God. Society feels the benefit. Places are blessed, not just people.

One of the last revivals in the British Isles occurred in the Hebrides just after World War 2. As Josh will report in the next chapter, certain individuals started to become very distressed by the lack of spiritual life on the islands and they got on their knees to pray. They started to take hold of God's promise in Isaiah 44:2-3.

> *This is what the Lord says -*
> *he who made you, who formed you in the womb,*
>   *and who **will** help you:*
> *Do not be afraid, Jacob, my servant,*
>   *Jeshurun, whom I have chosen.*
> *For I **will** pour water on the thirsty land,*
>   *and streams on the dry ground;*
> *I **will** pour out my Spirit on your offspring,*
>   *and my blessing on your descendants.*

Let's look at these magnificent verses.

Firstly, notice these words are a promise. I have put in bold the word "will". When God makes a promise, he also promises to keep it. He is our perfect Father. Like a perfect father, he intends to see his promises fulfilled. All he's looking for is people who have faith in the Promise Keeper. As Charles Spurgeon said in a wonderful sermon on this passage, "You have God's word for it; place your finger upon it, and on your knees beseech the Lord to do as he has said. He cannot lie, he never will revoke his word."[1]

Secondly, notice how God twice says "I" will. He does not wait for anyone else's permission. When he makes a decree, he does so as the King of kings. When he promises to send an outpouring of the Holy Spirit, we know it will happen. Again, as Spurgeon puts it, "A promise of God is the essence of truth, the soul of certainty, the voice of faithfulness, and the substance of blessing… When the season for spring has arrived, the Lord does not ask man to help him to remove the ice from the streams, or the snow from the hills, or the damps from the air. He asks no human aid in quickening the seeds, and arousing the plants, so that the sleeping flowers may open their lovely eyes and smile on all around. He does it all." This is true for revival too.

Thirdly, look at the impact zone of the promised outpouring of the Holy Spirit according to these verses. Revival will transform the environment. Thirsty lands and dry ground will be inundated. Just as wide-ranging, revival will also lead to our offspring and descendants being utterly transformed. This suggests children and young people will be especially impacted, although the promise of Pentecost (not just young men seeing visions, but old men dreaming dreams) reminds us that in every awakening people of all ages will be saved, and in very large numbers. As Spurgeon puts it, "We want more of the Spirit of God, and if we had it, I have no doubt whatever the converts would at once be counted by thousands and tens of thousands; and there is no reason whatever why the church of God, which is now in a pitiful minority, should not become in many a district a triumphant majority, and the influences of the grace of God be felt far and near."

So, the promises of God are for individuals, yes, but when it comes to the promises of God for revival, the plan of God is not just to forgive individuals for their sins but to heal the land. His purposes are to change the hearts of individuals and through these transformed individuals to redeem entire communities and even the earth itself. This is precisely what happened in the Hebridean revival. Hundreds of lost people, most notably young people, encountered the grace of God in a powerful, experiential, life-changing way. In this, God fulfilled his promise to forgive people for their sins. But there was so much more than this. The land itself was dramatically affected as well. Those who witnessed these heady days of the Spirit told of the fields and hills being illuminated at night by a blue phosphorescent light as the earth around them became ablaze with the knowledge of the glory of God, in fulfilment of yet another great Bible promise (Habakkuk 2:14). We should never underestimate the scope of God's promises.

THE POWER OF PROPHECY

It is important at this point to say that the promises of God for revival come not just through the written words of Scripture but also through the spoken words of those who have the gift of prophecy. Yes, the Hebridean revival came about as a direct result of people taking hold of God's promises in Isaiah 43:2-3 and reminding their Heavenly Father that he is a promise-keeping God. But in other revivals, the stimulus for believing in an imminent outpouring of the Spirit has come through prophetic words and visions. These did not in any way contradict or overrule the words of the Bible. True prophecy is always in agreement with the Word of God. But at the same time, prior to seasons of great awakening there have often been words and visions given by the Holy Spirit to key figures in the drama of what was to follow, and these prophetic phenomena have often taken on the nature of a promise from God's heart for a spiritual awakening.

Let's take the Welsh Revival of 1904. The central protagonist of that story of revival was a young man called Evan Roberts. In October of that year, he attended a revival meeting with his friend Sydney Evans. The preacher at the meeting, a man called Joseph Jenkins, preached on "How to Win Souls for Christ." Roberts was energised by this message. On the way home, he had a conversation with his friend that turned out to be a defining moment.[2]

"Do you think that it is too much to ask God to save one hundred thousand in Wales?"

"No," Sydney replied. "It would not be too much to ask God to save Wales and the world."

"Well, then," Evan said, "we must go at it earnestly."

A few nights later, Sydney woke up to discover that Evan Roberts was awake, and his face appeared to be glowing.

"Sid, I've got wonderful news for you," Roberts cried. "I had a vision of all Wales lifted to heaven. We are going to see the mightiest revival that Wales has ever known, and the Holy Spirit is coming just now. We must get ready. We must have a little band and go over all the country preaching."

As they marvelled at God's word to them, they were both looking up at the moon in the night sky. Both these young men had the same vision of God's hand reaching down from the moon to Wales and took this as confirmation that God was going to fulfil his promise and give them one hundred thousand souls. They would have this vision again, and on one occasion the hand of the Lord would be holding a piece of paper with the number 100,000 written on it.

The rest is history. Evan Roberts went about Wales preaching the same message. 1. We must confess before God every sin in our past life that has not been confessed. 2. We must remove anything that is doubtful in our lives. 3. Total Surrender. We must say and do all that the Spirit tells us. 4. Make a public confession of Christ. There was a mighty outpouring of the Holy Spirit and a great awakening in Wales. It is estimated that about one hundred thousand people gave their lives to Christ during this season. It is also worth remembering that the First World War broke out ten years later and that many of these saved young men perished on the battlefields of France. God knew what hard days lay ahead and determined that many of those who would meet their end in these tragic times should first have found peace with him. We can see the same dynamic playing out in the late 1850s in North America. Tens of thousands of men who were saved during the days of the New York Prayer Revival (a revival that swept throughout the USA and even to the UK and beyond) met their end in the terrible carnage of the American Civil War that followed on its heels.

GOOD NEWS STORIES (DEBRA)

WHAT WILL REVIVAL LOOK LIKE?

Evan Roberts was a man who leaned on the Holy Spirit for both the *vision* and the *strategy* for revival in Wales. We need to understand the difference between these two words, *vision* and *strategy*, if we are to see revival in our times. Vision is essentially what you see coming to pass in the future. It's a picture of what you see God doing. Strategy is what you need to do to get from where you are now to where God wants to take you. To put it as succinctly as possible, vision is the *what* and strategy is the *how*. Evan Roberts's vision was to see God save one hundred thousand souls in Wales. His strategy was the four points that he preached everywhere and which I have just mentioned. He said that preaching these simple four points was a plan given to him by the Holy Spirit. Both the vision and strategy were God-breathed.

What about revival in the 21st century?

What's the vision?

What's the strategy?

We have already talked about the impact zone of revival. God promises to forgive people their sins and to heal the land. We can therefore say that what we envision in the future is a move of God's Holy Spirit in which individuals are soundly converted and in which society is profoundly changed. In the Welsh Revival, one hundred thousand people were soundly converted. Many of these were men who worked underground in the coalmines of Wales. These miners lived most of their lives in the dark – literally and figuratively. They were so rough that their pit ponies were frightened of them. But when these men heard the Gospel, they repented of their sins and chose to follow the way of Jesus. Their transformation was so radical that the pit ponies at first didn't know how to respond to their handlers. They were used to being abused. Now they were being spoken to with kindness.

What I envision in the future is a combination of two things – countless individuals being saved, and society being transformed. I want to see people receive forgiveness for their sins, and I want to see the land healed. That said, I also acknowledge that God cannot be confined to the way he has done things in the past. Even though my heart's cry is, "Do it again, Lord!" I am not praying, "Do it again in the same way!" While my faith is uplifted by stories of past revivals, I wholly accept that when it comes to the strategy – the *how* – God's word to us may very well be, "Forget the former things!" (Isaiah 43:18). And "Behold, I am doing a new thing!" (Isaiah 43:19). We can learn from the past, but we must not and cannot be beholden to it, otherwise we may miss the day of God's visitation (Luke 19:44).

This is especially important if we are praying for and seeking a *sustainable* move of God. Many revivals in the past have petered out after a short while. A lot of this has been due to too much being expected of one person, usually an evangelist like Evan Roberts (Wales) or Duncan Campbell (the Hebrides). Instead of these men of faith remaining on fire they became burned out (even depressed in Roberts's case). This is not surprising when you remember that revivals such as those in Wales or the Hebrides were ones in which people gathered for meetings where the evangelist at the forefront of that move of God would preach the Gospel at great length. These gatherings would often go on until the early hours of the morning, causing many to become exhausted. This was never a sustainable model.

Josh and I have already spoken in this book about the variety of God's ways. Sometimes he moves suddenly, other times gradually. But we should also remember that when it comes to the outpouring of the Holy Spirit in revival, God also expects us to respect the fact that different times call for different ways.

What does this mean for the *how*? It means that we should respect the fact that places like the UK are now post-Christian. They are godless, secular mission fields where the levels of Christian understanding and biblical literacy are at an all-time low. If our strategy for revival is solely meetings-based, we may find that we get nowhere fast. People are less likely to be attracted to a gathering where the Gospel is preached because they have little to no idea of what that means, and little to no experience of stepping over the threshold into a religious space. No, it is far more likely that they will encounter God's kindness outside religious buildings or gatherings than they will inside these kinds of historic revival contexts. In other words, while gathering may still very much have its place, revival in the 21st century may well happen when Christians start dispersing, embracing a "go-to-them" more than a "come-to-us" strategy. As the writer of Ecclesiastes once told us, there are times and seasons for everything. Sometimes you need to gather the stones. Other times you need to scatter them (Ecclesiastes 3:3-5). Christians are living stones. We will need to be prepared to be dispersed with God's love burning in our hearts, bringing light to a post-Christian world living through a new and very dark age. Finding the right strategy for that will be crucial if revival is to be sustainable.

THE KING'S SPEECH

I'll never forget Martin Robinson, when he was with the Bible Society, asking, "How will you know when revival comes to a western 21st century context?" The answer? "When Good News stories are reported in the media."[3] If you think about it, that's likely to happen only when we as Christians understand that revival is for places not just people. Jonah came to understand that. God wanted Nineveh to be transformed. For that to happen, Jonah had to accept the call to be scattered or dispersed to a city he despised. See what happens when he does:

When Jonah's warning reached the king of Nineveh, he rose from his throne, took off his royal robes, covered himself with sackcloth and sat down in the dust. This is the proclamation he issued in Nineveh:
"By the decree of the king and his nobles:
Do not let people or animals, herds or flocks, taste anything; do not let them eat or drink. But let people and animals be covered with sackcloth. Let everyone call urgently on God. Let them give up their evil ways and their violence. Who knows? God may yet relent and with compassion turn from his fierce anger so that we will not perish."
When God saw what they did and how they turned from their evil ways, he relented and did not bring on them the destruction

he had threatened (Jonah 3:6-10).

Notice what happens when the King of Nineveh gets to hear what Jonah has been preaching. He issues a decree that everyone in his kingdom is to repent, just as he has. That's the equivalent of a modern-day king's speech. It's a broadcast message to the nation using the rudimentary communications media of his day.

Everything in the story of Jonah depended on him accepting the message to go when all he wanted to do was stay. Jonah would not have witnessed revival in Nineveh had he not repented, specifically for his initial refusal to go. Jonah 3, which describes the king's decree to the entire nation, begins with these words:

Then the word of the Lord came to Jonah a second time: "Go to the great city of Nineveh and proclaim to it the message I give you." Jonah obeyed the word of the Lord and went to Nineveh.

If we want to embrace God's strategy for revival in the 21st century, then we need to accept that this is far more likely to happen when we say yes to God's call to go where God calls us.

REDUCING CRIME

I have just quoted Martin Robinson saying that when the media reports our Good News stories that may be a sign that revival is in the air. I'd like to give an example of this from my own work.

Before we launched Redeeming Our Communities (ROC) in 2004, I led a movement called 'Prayer Network.' This involved churches of different denominations and streams praying together for societal transformation. In one of these city-wide prayer meetings, we gathered to pray for the police and for a reduction in crime. I interviewed a Christian police officer called Stephen Oake. I asked him why he had become a police officer, what it's like being a Christian in the police, and what his job looked like day to day. His answers opened our minds to the real issues the police are dealing with and how churches can support them not only in prayer but with practical action. When Stephen Oake was subsequently murdered in January 2003, his tragic death fuelled our desire and commitment to pray for the police.

ROC was launched in 2004 in the wake of our commitment to work alongside other organisations to promote safety. We held an event at the Reebok stadium which attracted 1500 attendees including the then Home Secretary, Hazel Blears. The focus was on churches getting behind the vision of reducing crime. Many officers from Greater Manchester Police (GMP) and the Merseyside Police attended. Following the event, street pastors and other practical initiatives were launched across the city. As our partnership with the GMP continued to grow, we held a large event at the Velodrome to address gang violence. Manchester by then had been nicknamed 'Gunchester'.

Hundreds of churches lent their support to the campaign and over 5000 people attended the event. The event was headline news on the BBC. The story was told under the heading, 'Thousands of Christians Praying about Gang

Violence.'[4] Josh was at this event having just come back to the Lord that year. He asked me if he could pray from the main platform. He then grabbed the microphone and prayed, "No more Gunchester! In the name of Jesus, I declare that our city will lose its Gunchester reputation and crime will be reduced!'

I remember being slightly concerned about Josh's boldness, especially as we had nine chief constables in attendance, including Sir Peter Fahy who was about to become the new chief of GMP.

I needn't have worried.

Six months later, on 29th January 2009, one newspaper headline read, "Is this the end of Gunchester?" That was the Manchester Evening News. David Ottewell wrote: "Manchester is on the brink of shedding its 'Gunchester' image for good after the astonishing success of a crackdown on the city's gangs. Only three shots were fired by gangsters between Valentine's Day in February and December 31st last year compared to more than 10 times as many in 2007. It is the first time since the height of Manchester's bloody street warfare in the early 1990s that entire months have passed in places like Moss Side without the sound of gunfire. Home Secretary Jacqui Smith will today travel to Manchester to hail the city's progress as an example to the rest of Britain - and pledge extra cash so the work can continue."[5]

Our relationship with GMP continued to develop and the first after-school ROC Café was opened by Sir Peter Fahy in 2009 in Reddish. The first three ROC Cafes were reported to have reduced ASB (antisocial behaviour) by an average of 45%.

The event at the Velodrome led to us doing a similar event

at the Echo Arena in 2009 following the tragic murders of Rhys Jones and Anthony Walker on Merseyside. 5000 people gathered as we promoted ways people to work together towards a safer society.

ROC went on to pioneer a restorative justice project in Manchester with Assistant Chief Constable Garry Shewan. This is now in its tenth year. We have been commissioned by the mayor's office to run restorative justice projects across Manchester. Many of our volunteers are from local churches. We have successfully dealt with hundreds of cases that have kept first-time offenders out of the criminal justice system. For this we received the RSQM (the Restorative Service Quality Mark) national award. In 2018 we were awarded the Queen's Award for voluntary service having successfully trained thousands of volunteers as mentors and community project leaders.

The simple model we developed in Manchester is now working across the UK as ROC has developed partnerships with other police forces. Recently, I spoke at the Christian Police Association's national leader's conference. It was amazing to see how ROC is working with police services across the UK and how local churches have become agents of change in keeping communities safe.

RIVERS OF FIRE

While it was mainly newspapers and TV carried our Good News stories back then, today the internet is the dominant means of communication. The worldwide web has created a massive network which allows the instant dissemination of information at the touch of a screen or keyboard. The ease and speed with which this can now happen means that revival news can be transmitted throughout the globe in a matter of seconds. What in former times would have taken years can now take the time you need to read this sentence.

One of the most powerful prophecies of revival was given to Jean Darnell in 1967.[6] She saw the British Isles covered in a green haze. As she looked, pinpoints of light began to pierce through the mist. These were fires breaking out all over the nation, from Scotland in the north, to Land's End in the south. When these God-lit fires were joined together, they began to increase in brightness.

As Jean continued to pray, she saw lightning, explosions of fire, and then rivers of fire flowing from north to south - from Scotland, Ireland, and Wales into England. Some of these streams of fire crossed the channel into Europe while others stopped. As Jean asked God what this meant, he showed her that these fires were pockets of people who had been made intensely hungry for the Word of God and for New Testament Christianity. These were people who had read the Book of Acts and wondered, *where is this church?*

Jean asked God for more revelation, and he told her that they pointed to two moves of the Holy Spirit that he was promising to the UK in the future. The first would be a renewal of Christian faith, including the fullness of the Holy Spirit within the church. This has, without question, been happening over the last sixty years. The second was this: the renewal of life within the church would spread outside its walls resulting in a public awakening impacting every level of the nation's life –

schools, university campuses, colleges, media, government, etc. There would be so many conversions that it would change the character of the nation and determine a future move of God in Europe. There would not be a sphere of the nation's life that would not feel the impact of the awakening when God releases it to the country. Has this occurred yet? We need to be honest and answer no. We are still waiting for a national revival in the UK.

Then she added something very significant.

The word 'communicators' was laid on Jean's heart - a word that was not fashionable in those days. Indeed, the internet was not invented until nearly three decades later. Jean explained that as the rivers of fire moved, it would produce powerfully gifted communicators who would address others through the media - the arts, journalism, radio, TV, and so on. Actors, singers, teachers, and powerful communicators (those who have an anointing to work through the media) will be the new warriors that the Lord uses. They will mainly be from the younger generation, and they will be used by God to reach people in Europe. They will be excellent in all they do and will work with others of similar calibre in Europe to release God's Word *speedily*. This will result in another wave of awakening.

What a vision that is!

And what a strategy!

A sustainable one too.

Josh and I want to see anointed communicators raised by God for such a time as this – people with the fire of his Holy Spirit burning in their hearts, people with an excellence in communication telling God's Good news stories through traditional media like TV and newspapers, and through the new media like TikTok, Instagram, and YouTube. God inspired the inventors of the printing press in the fifteenth century and established a new technology then. In the following century, this technology carried the Good News stories of the reformation. In a not dissimilar way, the invention of the internet in the twentieth century has established a new technology that can carry the Good News stories of revival far and wide in this present century.

Nothing is an accident.

God is still on his throne.

He truly is our Promise Keeper.

What we need to do is take hold of the promises of God and pray with heartfelt faith for him to fulfil his Word. As Charles Spurgeon concluded in the sermon I quoted earlier, "Plead more earnestly in private, make your prayer-meetings more energetic, attend them more numerously, throw your hearts more fully into them, and God's Spirit will be surely given."

Amen to that!

FOOTNOTES

1. Charles Spurgeon, 'A Promise for us and for our Children' (1864), https://www.spurgeon.org/resource-library/sermons/a-promise-for-us-and-for-our-children/#flipbook/

2. For Evan Roberts's testimony, see https://revival-library.org/revival-resources/for-revival-seekers/revival-tips-from-history/evan-roberts-keys-of-revival/

3. Martin Robinson, Formerly Bible Society. Debra heard Martin Robinson preach in Southampton.

4. http://news.bbc.co.uk/1/hi/england/manchester/7432998.stm

5. David Ottewell. Manchester Evening News Headline, 'Is this the end of Gunchester?' David Ottewell 29/1/2009.

6. Jean Darnell. Jean had this vision three times. See https://www.byfaith.co.uk/paulrevival4.htm

CHAPTER 7

YOUR HONOUR IS AT STAKE! (JOSH)

Not long ago, I made the long journey to the Hebrides where a great revival broke out in 1949. I visited the small cottage in the village of Barvas where two elderly women of prayer, Peggy and Christine Smith, once lived.[1] They were eighty-four and eighty-two years old at the time of the outpouring of the Holy Spirit. It is believed that one of the sisters was blind, the other almost crippled by arthritis. Their age and condition meant that they weren't well enough to attend public worship services, so they resolved to pray in their humble cottage. They prayed that God would fulfil the Biblical promise that Mum looked at in the last chapter: "I will pour water on the thirsty land, and streams on the dry ground; I will pour out my Spirit on your offspring, and my blessing on your descendants" (Isaiah 44:3).

Peggy and Christine prayed every Tuesday and Thursday evening from 10pm-3am (and I think that I'm sometimes too tired to pray!) They had lived through revivals and become desperate for God to move again. They believed that God was going to keep his promises and that the church would be filled again with young people.

One day, they sent for an evangelist on the mainland of Scotland called Duncan Campbell. He told them he was too busy to come. They replied by giving him a rebuke, telling him that was what man had said, but God said otherwise! When Campbell changed his schedule and came to the Hebrides, the fire began to fall.[2]

As the revival was at its height, Peggy asked Campbell to go to a small, isolated village. The people there were quite defiant in their unwillingness to have revival meetings. Duncan was also hesitant, but Peggy persisted because God had given her a promise about that village. Peggy prayed, "Lord, you remember what you told me this morning, that in this village you are going to save seven men who will become pillars in the church of my fathers. Lord, I have given your message to Mister Campbell, and it seems he is not prepared to receive it. Oh Lord, give him wisdom, because he badly needs it!"[3]

Campbell ended up agreeing. When he arrived in the village at 7pm, he found to his amazement a large bungalow crowded to capacity. Many more were waiting outside the house. He began to preach, and when he finished, a minister asked him to counsel people who were grieving over their sins. Among them were Peggy's seven men![4]

Will we believe like Peggy that "God is not human, that he should lie, not a human being, that he should change his mind. Does he speak and then not act? Does he promise and not fulfil?" (Numbers 23:19). Will we believe God for revival?

And will we pray and work for an awakening that lasts for a long time, not just a season.

SOMETHING SUSTAINED

In 2009, a friend of mine called James Aladiran took me to the Ramp in a small town called Hamilton in the backwoods of Alabama - far from any major city. The Ramp started as a youth ministry with seven young people and their leader Karen Wheaton. She had grown up there and felt called to return. When she entered the town, she saw how aimless the young people were. They had no idea who God was. God made her a promise: "What you invest in the lives of other young people, you will reap in your own children."[5]

God started to work in the lives of the young people, moving mightily through their prayers. Since then, a 3-day Ramp conference has been taking place many times a year for over 25 years. Nearly one million young people have passed through their doors. Thousands have also gone through their ministry school, Ramp University, and countless lives have been radically changed. And I could see why. These young people were praying and fasting to awaken, equip, and send a generation. I had seen this same fire in James too. It was contagious.

One of my favourite expressions of James's is this: "You don't know you're asleep until you wake up!"[6] That was true for me. I was 19 at the time, and I'd been a Christian for almost two years. My road to meeting Jesus was interesting, as I've already shown, but I found myself in good company at the Ramp because many of the young people there had a similar story. They had woken up, to use James's phrase. In fact, what struck me was their intense hunger for Jesus. It was sincere, bold, captivating. There were three services a day. Most worship sets lasted two hours and every sermon one hour plus. The whole emphasis was not on entertainment but on encountering God. Everyone was completely focused on Jesus. Even people younger than me were single-minded for God. It was inevitable that all this would change me too.

The testimonies I heard in that place were spine-tingling – not just ones about coming to Jesus, but about staying devoted to him for life. This really struck me. The Ramp was not about temporary decisions; it was about permanent discipleship. It wasn't just about conversions; it was about consecration. There are thousands of stories from the Ramp of authentic, long-term, life-change.

Jesus told us to go into all the world and make disciples, not just decisions. Of course, discipleship starts with a decision to follow Jesus and continues with an everyday decision to keep following him, but I'm talking about the difference between a momentary and a lifelong yes. God gave Karen Wheaton a promise that he would move mightily in the lives of the young people in Hamilton. She held onto the promise and saw, and is still seeing, a move of God. And not just a short-term one either, but rather a revival that has stood the test of time. To use a word from my mum's previous chapter, it has been *sustained* because they resolved to make disciples, not just encourage decisions.

This is important. God promises revival, yes, but he wants

it to be something that's sustained not short-lived. Starting a revival is all about encounter. It's about experiencing how real God is. Sustaining revival is about discipleship. It's about making a choice to be fully devoted to Jesus every day for the rest of your life.

What I learned from my friend James and my time at the Ramp is this: discipleship ensures that the encounter experienced at the start of revival isn't short-lived but sustained. Saul being knocked off his horse and meeting Jesus is encounter. Saul becoming Paul and serving the purposes of God for his generation, being obedient to God's vision for the entire course of his life, that's discipleship. If we want to pray and work for a long-term move of God, we need both.

SOMETHING SENT

There's something else we need too. Early in 2023, my wife and I began following a story coming out of Asbury University in Kentucky. A small group of young people had stayed behind to pray after an ordinary chapel service. God started to move in their lives and this group grew bigger and bigger. Many of them were weeping and finding wholeness, freedom, and healing in the presence of Jesus. This was all led by the young people themselves, supported by spiritual leaders and staff. The hours turned to days and the hundreds turned to thousands. Many other college campuses in the USA reported similar stories.

Not long after reading the reports, I felt unable to stay at home. I had to be there, so I booked a flight and off I went. When I arrived at Asbury, I found myself standing at the back of Hughes Auditorium with tears streaming down my face as I watched young people giving everything to Jesus in hours of prayer and adoration. There were pockets of us who had travelled from the UK and Europe desperate to see something similar back home.

After a few days there, I got to know some of the men and women who'd been praying for a move of God on campus in the years leading up to this outpouring. One of the things that was most striking about them was that they were way more interested in the revival spreading than they were seeing thousands of people coming to Asbury. While they loved everything God was doing in Asbury, their hearts were turned outwards to the lost. This is in fact how Asbury University was founded. Frank Asbury was a circuit rider with the Methodist movement – a movement sparked by John Wesley in the 18th Century. Young people like Asbury had such a strong passion for sharing the Gospel that they'd ride thousands of miles on horseback. Asbury University was named after someone deeply committed to the lost.

After sixteen days, the Asbury meetings ended. I say "ended" but the team continued to disciple all those who were saved during the outpouring. Many other colleges around the USA are still experiencing wonderful things from mass baptisms to packed-out worship meetings. But back at Asbury, they decided to focus on sending rather than staying or sitting. They urged those that came to their meetings to take the presence of God back home. They knew this revival was for the world, that a move of God must, well, move!

When Jesus told his disciples to go into all the world, he

didn't expect them to respond by sitting and revelling in their own encounters with him. They could have held countless meetings and talked endlessly about all that Jesus did, but they would have missed the true reason why Jesus came - to seek and save the lost (Luke 19:10). Yes, meetings are important, but we're meant to be scattered as well as gathered, just as Mum said in the last chapter. And scattered means letting the world see how real God is. It means understanding that revival is something sent.

SOMETHING SEEN

In 2020, like many of us, I found myself scrolling endlessly through the internet. Christian ministries were reporting something happening with Gen Z; lots of videos were trending on Tik-Tok with young people sharing their faith, praying for certain issues, and quoting the Bible. Topics like 'Prayer for Anxiety', 'Prayer for my Family', 'How to Know Jesus', were filling the search engines. There were hundreds of videos. Some had millions of views.[7]

I couldn't quite believe it. Members of Gen Z were searching. The pain of losing their teenage years during the pandemic, and the mental health struggles they were experiencing too, seemed to drive them to look beyond themselves for answers. This gave birth to a great mission field ripe for harvest - the online space.

This online space is both exciting and daunting, complex and polarising. We must exercise wisdom and caution, but equally we can't be fearful. Our task is to enter this space with kindness and conviction, wisdom and winsomeness, courage and humility. Above all, we need to be creative. What are the ways we can engage with a new generation that's a captive audience? Young people are on their phones a lot, and it doesn't look like that is going to change. Look at these two quotes:

"Almost half of Gen Zs and Millennials in the US say they spend more time socialising with others in social media than in the physical world, and 40% admit to socialising more in video games than in the physical world."[8]

"More than half of Gen Zers spend nine hours or more in a typical day using their smartphones, and nearly half of them spend 3-8 hours per day on their smartphones."[9]

If young people all over the world are scrolling on their screens, how can we make sure they see how real God is?

We know young people spend a lot of time in school, so we have school's workers. They come to youth groups, so we have youth leaders. We also know that almost all young people spend a lot of time online, so that's why we need Christian content creators. Are we ready to make content that is excellent enough to catch their attention, deep enough to keep it, and powerful enough to ensure they encounter Jesus in meaningful ways? Romans 10:14 says, "How, then, can they call on the one they have not believed in? And how can they believe in the one of whom they have not heard? And how can they hear without someone preaching to them?" Good News stories need to be seen (demonstration) and heard (proclamation). Jesus said, "No one lights a lamp and hides it in a clay jar or puts it under a bed. Instead, they put it on a stand, so that those who come in can see the light" (Luke 8:16).

Didn't Jesus say that the whole world will hear his message before he returns? "And this gospel of the kingdom will be preached in the whole world as a testimony to all nations, and then the end will come." (Matthew 24:13). There has never been a time when this could be considered possible. Until now.

An outpouring of the Spirit is **sustained** by calling people to lifelong discipleship. This moves us from simply seeing things start to ensuring their longevity. We make sure we're not just lighting fires but collecting logs to keep the fire burning.

An outpouring of the Spirit becomes something **sent** when the Church keeps the main thing the main thing – in other words, the call to "presence and purpose," as one of my pastors Stacie Reeser often says.[10] We pursue God in prayer and then go into all the world with his power and make disciples just as Jesus instructed. This way we make sure we don't keep the blessings of revival to ourselves but take them to those who need to be awakened.

Finally, an outpouring of the Spirit is something **seen** not only in miracles and acts of mercy, but by us boldly, kindly, and intelligently utilising the online space to preach and demonstrate the Good News of Jesus to a generation scrolling and searching for meaning. People are there waiting for someone to reach them.

A MATTER OF THE HEART

If this **sustaining**, **sending**, and **seeing** is to happen, we must first allow God to do something in our hearts. Rick Warren says, "the heart of the matter is the matter of the heart." That's true. When we pray, God hears the words of our mouths, but he also sees the state of hearts. Our prayers and our worship ascend like an aroma before the Lord. If our prayers for revival are full of selfishness and greed, what fragrance will they have? Many people encourage us to pray, "God send revival and start with us." But what if the prayer we really should be praying is, "God send revival and do what you will"?

Here are some more questions. What if God doesn't want to start with us? What if he wants to start with the young people at Asbury? What if he wants to pour out his Spirit on online influencers and turn them into TikTok missionaries? What if he wants to use Christian artists to populate the world with consecrated creativity? Are our hearts prepared for this? What if revival looked like all churches filled, not just ours? What if revival looked like all nations hearing the gospel, not just our own? My friend Aaron Nayagam says, "if the Lord answered all your prayers today, would it change the world, or just yours?"[11]

Think of the great prophecy that Joel gave in the Old Testament. Everyone loves the bit where God promises to pour out his Spirit:

I will pour out my Spirit on all people.
Your sons and daughters will prophesy,
　your old men will dream dreams,
　your young men will see visions.
Even on my servants, both men and women,
　I will pour out my Spirit in those days.

That's in Joel 2:28-29. But we should never forget that this promise was preceded by a call to do something about our hearts.

> *"Even now," declares the Lord,*
>   *"return to me with all your heart,*
>   *with fasting and weeping and mourning."*
> *Rend your heart*
>   *and not your garments.*
> *Return to the Lord your God,*
>   *for he is gracious and compassionate,*
> *slow to anger and abounding in love,*
>   *and he relents from sending calamity.*

That's in verses 12-13. It's followed by this call:

> *"Blow the trumpet in Zion,*
>   *declare a holy fast,*
>   *call a sacred assembly.*
> *Gather the people,*
>   *consecrate the assembly;*
> *bring together the elders,*
>   *gather the children,*
>   *those nursing at the breast.*
> *Let the bridegroom leave his room*
>   *and the bride her chamber.*
> *Let the priests, who minister before the Lord,*
>   *weep between the portico and the altar.*
> *Let them say, 'Spare your people, Lord'."*

FIVE CONDITIONS FOR REVIVAL

We love the fact that God is a Promise Keeper, but we don't always love how his promises are to be kept, because he often works with and within us to bring them about. And that is normally costly! What we see in passages like Joel 2 is the kind of prayer God calls for when he is seeking to pour out his Spirit. He calls for us to engage in a kind of praying that purifies our hearts and our motives.

Firstly, he calls for **repentance**. It's hard to miss the summons to repentance in Joel chapter 2, but what we may miss is the form this repentance is to take. Weeping and mourning, wearing sackcloth and ashes, are not commonplace in worship services today, but what they point to is something truly heartfelt – what in 2 Corinthians 7:10 Paul calls "godly sorrow." Perhaps we've lost sight of the importance of mourning because we've become so accustomed to quoting Romans 2:4: "the kindness of God leads you to repentance." We tend to focus solely on kindness, and, in the process, we forget the other side of the coin, the Biblical idea of broken-hearted grief over sin.

At the beginning of this chapter, I mentioned the Hebridean revival of 1949-1952. This outpouring of the Spirit was preceded by women praying for revival. They called for the men to do the same. As the men prayed, they were drawn to Psalm 24:3-4:

"Who may ascend the mountain of the Lord? Who may stand in his holy place? The one who has clean hands and a pure heart, who does not trust in an idol or swear by a false god."

One of the men began to cry out to God. "Oh God, are my hands clean? Is my heart pure?" He then fell to the floor.

At that very moment, the story goes that people from across the region began to wake suddenly in the night and make their way to the church to get right with God![12] Repentance is indispensable to revival. We must take the low road if we're to experience the mountaintop moments of God pouring out his Spirit.

The second thing we learn from Joel 2 is the need for **returning**. Returning is perhaps the next step after repentance, although I don't want this whole thing to sound like steps or formulae to revival. If repentance is about getting right with God again, returning is about coming back to a right way of relating to God. It's about seeing God as our first and foremost priority.

My friend Matt Wilson from Prayer Storm says, "In the modern church we often have the most important commandments the wrong way round; we seem to prioritise loving people at the expense of loving God. But you can't love God properly until you love him first."[13] I would add that we can't love people properly either until we love God first. And this is what returning is all about. We make ministering to God our main agenda, and ministry to others flows from it. As Joel puts it, I resolve to "minister before the altar," to "minister before my God." I resolve to put ministering *to* God before ministering *for* God.

Only those who have an intense hunger for God can be said to fulfil the condition of returning. Joel talks about fasting, weeping, and mourning which suggest desperation. This reminds me of the words of St. Augustine: "without God we cannot; without us, God will not." This is part of the complex nature of revival. In one sense God doesn't need us at all, yet he involves us anyway, and it seems our part is significant. In the same way we can't act like this all revolves around us. We also cannot camp out in complacency either; we must be consecrated and committed to the cause – God's agenda for the earth. Returning is therefore not about locking ourselves away from the world. It's what leads us to being authorised and anointed to reach it most effectively. This is the power source for engaging with a lost world.

The third condition for revival involves **restoring** – that is, restoring our meetings in the house of God to something solemn and sacred. One of the things that struck me the most when I visited Asbury was a large sign above the stage. It read, "Holiness unto the Lord." This formed a holy summons over everything that was said and done in that place. It set the tone for everything and was a continual reminder to everyone that God should be respected and honoured, that the place we were in was not just a room but a sanctuary.

The chapel at Asbury was built within the Methodist tradition started by John Wesley, perhaps the greatest revival preacher in British history. Holiness was something that John Wesley held as foundational for God's people. This is what Joel was urging, and it's what we see so often being emphasized throughout revival history. Revival preachers such as John Wesley in England, Evan Roberts in Wales, and Duncan Campbell in Scotland, all urged their listeners to cultivate a fear for the Lord and a reverence for God's house. In fact, this is what caused many to repent and turn back to God in the first place.

Reflecting on the Hebridean revival, Duncan Campbell said this: "When God stepped down, suddenly men, and women all over the parish, were gripped by the fear of God."[14] Don't think this means that church meetings were suddenly quiet and joyless. Weeping and wailing isn't exactly silent business. And according to the Bible, weeping is temporary. "There may be tears in the night, but there will be joy in the morning" (Psalm 30:5). In fact, one of the passages most quoted during the Hebridean revival was Psalm 126:

> *When the Lord restored the fortunes of Zion,*
> * we were like those who dreamed.*
> *Our mouths were filled with laughter,*
> * our tongues with songs of joy.*
> *Then it was said among the nations,*
> * "The Lord has done great things for them."*
> *The Lord has done great things for us,*
> * and we are filled with joy.*

It is possible to have a solemn and sacred assembly that weeps and rejoices, mourns and laughs, prays with serious conviction and praises with wild exuberance. Romans 12:15 calls us to both: "Rejoice with those who rejoice, weep with those who weep."

The fourth element Joel proposes is a matter of **rending** - rending our hearts, that is. The kind of rending is not something commonly seen in the modern church. To rend means to "cause great emotional pain to our hearts." In a world where a lot of people are already in pain, this may not seem like an attractive call at all, but I think Joel is referring here to something that ends up blessing us and others. He's referring to us choosing to allow our hearts to be broken by the things that break God's heart. In other words, he's urging us to carry a God-given intercessory burden for others, especially those who are lost.

When we rend our hearts, we're making ourselves available for God to remove what is a heart of stone and replace it with a heart of flesh in us (Ezekiel 36:26). We're asking God to fill us with his Spirit and his will so we can pray, "Let your kingdom come, let your will be done" (Luke 11:2). Seen this way, the biblical idea of rending our hearts is not negative or miserable. It's something that draws us closer to God and makes us more like him. Why? Because as someone once beautifully put it, "When you look closely into the heart of God, you'll see a Cross-shaped scar." Remember, in Luke 9:23, Jesus says, "Whoever wants to be my disciple must deny themselves and take up their cross daily and follow me." While carrying the cross represents a dying to self, it can also mean carrying God's broken heart for the world.

The fifth and final call Joel sets out for us is what I call **responding** - I mean responding in prayer. The word 'prayer' is not explicitly mentioned in Joel 2, though it is implied and called for, and prayers are recorded within it. The outpouring of prayer from us often precedes the outpouring of God's Spirit on us. This is a crucial part of the point Joel is making in chapter 2. God promises to pour out his Spirit on us when we return to him with passionate, repentant hearts, pleading for him to visit us again. When we rend our hearts, he rends the heavens.

We can see this in Acts 2 as the early church gathers before the Day of Pentecost. The 120 disciples in Jerusalem meet regularly to pray for the Holy Spirit to come. Jesus promised them that if they did this, they would receive the gift the Father promised – namely the power of the Spirit. When they pray, the promise is fulfilled. The Spirit comes like fire from heaven, and they're filled with the power of God. Peter, inspired by the Spirit, quotes the Book of Joel, specifically chapter 2, and tells the marvelling crowd that this is in fulfilment of what the Father promised in the Scriptures.

Prayer is what precedes the outpouring of the Spirit on the Day of Pentecost, and it is prayer that precedes the outpourings of the Spirit in revival history. This is a principle that preachers often mention. It's almost a cliché to say that every great move of God begins with a great move of prayer. We may have heard John Wesley's remark, "God does nothing except in response to believing prayer."[15] It's one thing to say it. It's quite another to do it. Are we responding in prayer? Are we doing what the 120 disciples did and calling on our Heavenly Father to answer the prayer that he always loves to answer – the prayer for more of his tangible presence among us? Are we prepared to prioritise these five fundamental calls we see in Joel chapter 2?

Repentance – confessing where we have gone wrong and getting right with God.

Returning - to our first love, loving God before anyone or anything, then loving others from that place.

Restoring - the church to what Joel calls a solemn and sacred assembly, characterised by holiness and reverence, leading to joy.

Rending - allowing the Holy Spirit to break our hearts for this lost and broken world.

Responding - by praying for the gift the Father promised, the outpouring of the Holy Spirit.

When we do these things, I am convinced that what ascends from our hearts and our mouths will have a fragrance that is holy and acceptable to God. Both the Word of God and the testimonies from past revivals reassure us that when we make this kind of offering, God keeps his promises. He is a Promise-Keeping God, and when we sincerely follow how God wants to fulfil his promises – such as we find in passages like Joel 2 and 2 Chronicles 7:14 – then we find that God fulfils his Word and strikes the earth with revival fire.

BACK TO THE HEBRIDES

When I visited the Hebrides, I was told first-hand about how the revival was not well received by some of the churches there. My friend Matthew MacNeil, a youth pastor in Stornoway (the capital of the Isle of Lewis), told me that the revival never reached the main city on the island and was rejected by most of its churches.

One evening, when the opposition got all too much for those involved in the revival, a prayer meeting was called. Around midnight Duncan Campbell turned to the local blacksmith. "John, I feel the time has come for you to pray."

John, a giant of a man, rose to pray in a loud and bold voice. He raised his right hand to heaven as he spoke. "Oh God, you made a promise to pour water upon him that is thirsty and floods upon the dry ground. And, Lord, it's not happening." He paused before continuing. "Lord, I don't know how the others here stand in your presence, I don't know how the ministers stand, but, Lord, if I know anything about my own heart, I stand before thee as an empty vessel, thirsting for thee and for a manifestation of thy power." He halted again, and after a moment of tense silence, he thundered, "Oh God, your honour is at stake, and I now challenge you to fulfil your covenant engagement and do what you have promised to do."[16]

Here was a man who took seriously the fact that we can boldly approach God's throne (Hebrews 4:16). Here was a man who prayed what Jeremiah prayed. "Your reputation is at stake! Don't quit on us! Don't walk out and abandon your glorious Temple! Remember your covenant. Don't break faith with us!" (Jeremiah 14:21, *The Message*). Here was a man who prayed like Hezekiah prays in 2 Kings 19:19: "Now, LORD our God, deliver us from his hand, so that all the kingdoms of the earth may know that you alone, LORD, are God."

The story goes that after the blacksmith prayed, the house where they were standing began to shake. Dishes rattled, tables and chairs vibrated, and the people were shell-shocked. Some who witnessed this likened it to Acts 4:31: "After they prayed, the place where they were meeting was shaken. And they were all filled with the Holy Spirit and spoke the word of God boldly."[17]

TIME TO SHINE

And that's an important place to end this chapter. When God poured out his Spirit in Acts 4 it was for a reason. He wanted his people to speak the message clearly and courageously to a lost world. Remember what Jesus promised in Acts 1:8:

"You will receive power when the Holy Spirit comes on you; and you will be my witnesses in Jerusalem, and in all Judea and Samaria, and to the ends of the earth."

We should not miss the importance of the word 'witness'. In the original Greek language of Acts, the noun translated 'witness' is *martus* (a person who witnesses) from which we get 'martyr.' While many of us may not be called to martyrdom, we are challenged by stories of those who are to go all-in for our faith. Their witness inspires ours. It calls us to wholehearted devotion; even if we don't lose our lives, there are other costs we must count. God does not give us the power of his Spirit so that we can keep the blessing to ourselves but to give his blessings to the whole world. We need this divine power if we are going to give a clear and compelling testimony about Jesus to people in our city (Jerusalem), in our region (Judea), in nearby countries (Samaria), and the world (the ends of the earth).

As Mum wrote in the last chapter, when it comes to God as our Promise Keeper, the impact zone is more about communities and societies than it is about individuals alone. God promises to pour out his Spirit on thirsty ground and dry land. He wants what he promises to go into all the world and to the ends of the earth.

What greater incentive could we have to take up our cross and deny ourselves? What greater reward could we have for not only praying the promises of God but living them too? God has promised that he will pour out his Spirit again. He has told us through great warriors of prayer like Jean Darnell that he wants to visit the British Isles with the fire of his Spirit. It's time for us to see the pinpricks of light breaking through the haze that covers this country. It's time for these lights to join and for churches to come alive again, as they have in places as far apart as the Hebrides and Hamilton. It's time for the anointed communicators to arise and enter the online mission field with God's Good News stories. As we will see in the final part of this book, it's time for the light bringers to dispel the darkness that covers the earth. It's truly a time for God's people to shine.

FOOTNOTES

1. Colin and Mary Peckham, *Sounds from Heaven: The Revival on the Isle of Lewis*, 1949-1952. Christian Focus; First Edition (2004), p.111.

2. *Sounds from Heaven*, p.37. Campbell makes it clear that revival preceded his arrival but he – along with many others - also acknowledged that there were great breakthroughs and an increase of God's Spirit when he came to the Hebrides.

3. https://ctntp.uk/other-insights/the-intercessors-of-the-hebrides-revival/

4. https://ctntp.uk/other-insights/the-intercessors-of-the-hebrides-revival/

5. https://karenwheaton.com/the-ramp/

6. https://www.bible.com/reading-plans/53573-life-on-fire/day/1

7. Brian Barcelona shares about how he moved to doing online ministry due to Covid and that his ministry grew from reaching thousands to millions in a matter of months. https://mycharisma.com/article/gen-z-evangelist-brian-barcelona-how-the-covid-shutdown-led-to-a-digital-missions-movement-of-seismic-proportions/

8. https://www.prnewswire.com/news-releases/the-quest-for-connection-younger-generations-look-to-user-generated-content-and-video-games-to-find-value-meaning-and-personal-fulfillment-301798079.html

9. https://www.davidpublisher.com/index.php/Home/Article/index?id=41256.html#:~:text=The%20results%20revealed%20that%20almost,per%20day%20on%20their%20smartphones

10. Stacie Reeser, https://www.youtube.com/watch?v=FX4MUgnoS5k&themeRefresh=1

11. Aaron Nayagam, https://www.youtube.com/watch?v=fTANmt0kHdI

12. *Sounds from Heaven*, p.56.

13. Matt says this in many of his sermons. https://www.worldinvisible.com/library/wesley/8317/831711.htm

14. *Sounds from Heaven*, p.113.

15. John Wesley, in chapter 11 of his book, *A Plain Account of Christian Perfection*. See, https://www.worldinvisible.com/library/wesley/8317/831711.htm

16. *Sounds from Heaven*, p.113.

17. *Sounds from Heaven*, p.113.

PART 4
LIGHT BRINGER

CHAPTER 8
REDEEMING OUR COMMUNITIES (DEBRA)

When I was a little girl at primary school in Kent, we were asked to do a project on someone we admired. I chose the 19th century nurse and celebrity, Florence Nightingale. Florence Nightingale is best known as 'the Lady with the Lamp' and the founder of modern nursing. She was born on 12th May 1820 in the Italian city of Florence – a city after which she was named. Growing up in an influential and wealthy British family, it became clear from an early age that Florence was devoted to helping others. By the time she was 17, she was talking about having experienced a call of God to spend the rest of her life devoted to the service of others. As she sought to begin her life's purpose, she endured opposition from family members who were eager for her to do what was expected of women of her social standing and become a dutiful wife and mother. Florence ignored this pressure and worked hard to educate herself in the science and practice of nursing.

Thirteen years later, Florence started to engage in the work with which she is now associated. In 1850, she found herself in Germany visiting a Lutheran religious community. Seeing how the sisters looked after the sick with compassion and commitment, she was inspired by their example. This was the turning point in her life. She stayed in the community and received four months training in medical care. Several years later, she became superintendent of the Institute for the Care of Sick Gentlewomen in Harley Street. When the Crimean War broke out, Sydney Herbert, Secretary of War, recruited her to travel to Scutari to serve the wounded and sick soldiers at the military hospital. What she found there horrified her. There was a lack of hygiene and medicines, the diet was poor, the atmosphere foul, and many suffered from fatal infections. As a result of her petitioning *The Times*, Isambard Kingdom Brunel, the famous engineer, was commissioned to build a prefabricated hospital which was shipped to the Dardanelles. Within a short time, the number of deaths had been reduced from 42% to 2%.

It was during her work at Scutari that Florence gained the nickname 'the Lady with the Lamp.' *The Times* reported that at night she would walk among the beds, checking the wounded men holding a light in her hand. A report described her in glowing terms (quite literally): "She is a 'ministering angel' without any exaggeration in these hospitals, and as her slender form glides quietly along each corridor, every poor fellow's face softens with gratitude at the sight of her. When all the medical officers have retired for the night and silence and darkness have settled down upon those miles of prostrate sick, she may be observed alone, with a little lamp in her hand, making her solitary rounds.' This image of 'the Lady with the Lamp' captured the public's imagination and Florence became a celebrity. The poet Longfellow further popularized it in a poem 1857 ('Santa Filomena').

Florence Nightingale's influence was immense. Her example and teaching inspired the belief that nurses, by personality and training, should not sit on the sidelines watching. Nightingale fought to have nurses lead, not just follow. Thanks largely to her, the profession of nursing started to gain the respect it deserved. She is also remembered as a reformer of hospital sanitation methods. For most of her ninety years, she pushed for an improvement in the British military health-care system. She made innovative use of new techniques of statistical analysis, such as during the Crimean War when she plotted the incidence of needless deaths caused by unsanitary conditions and created a pathway for change. She proved that social phenomena could be objectively measured and subjected to mathematical analysis. She was a pioneer in the collection, tabulation, interpretation, and graphical display of descriptive statistics.

The achievements of the Lady with the Lamp were astonishing when you consider that most Victorian women from her background did not attend universities or pursue professional careers. Her father, William Nightingale, believed women – including his children - should get an education, so Florence learned Italian, Latin, Greek, history, and mathematics. This empowered her to collect data and systematise record-keeping practices at Scutari. She set about the task of improving city and military hospitals by representing the data graphically. This ability to collate and communicate provided an organized way of learning and led to improvements in medical practices. She then developed a model Hospital Statistical Form for nurses to collect and generate consistent data and statistics. She became a fellow of the Royal Statistical Society in 1858 and an honorary member of the American Statistical Association in 1874. She has been called a 'prophetess' in the development of applied statistics.

A PASSION FOR JUSTICE

Why do I do what I do now? Why do I have such a passion for justice? Why do I want to make a difference in society? As I look back, I can see that the project I did on Florence Nightingale at school was something of a turning point for me. I can see how her example helped me to believe that I too could be a person who could change things for the better. When I became a Christian in 1980, I was in my early twenties. This strengthened my sense of purpose. I am not in any way likening myself to Florence Nightingale. I am not a nurse, and I faint at the mere sight of blood. However, I do relate to being a woman called to a position of leadership within a social and religious context which has not always approved of female leaders. I also relate to being determined, to never giving up on your God-given dream.

As we have just celebrated twenty years of my charity, Redeeming Our Communities (ROC), I can see all sorts of ways that God's light has shone in dark places. What we do is founded on the idea that we can be light bearers in the place God positions us, responding to the needs we see around us. Jesus said, "I am the light of the world" (John 8:12), but he also said to his disciples, "Let your light shine before others, so that they may see your good works and give glory to your Father in heaven" (Matthew 5:16, CSB).

There are many areas of darkness in UK society today. I wrote earlier in this book about the city of Manchester having the nickname 'Gunchester' in the 1980s and 90s. But there are other harrowing challenges besides guns. Loneliness, what Mother Teresa referred to as the leprosy of the West, is at an all-time high. Loneliness is a crippling condition, leaving people feeling isolated and alienated from society. Loneliness even impacts our physical health; it is said to be as bad for us as smoking fifteen cigarettes a day.

Then there's the growing problem of mental health. In 2023-24, 21.8 million people in the UK contacted mental health services, a 9.4% increase from the previous year. Nearly one quarter of young people aged 16-24 say their mental health is bad. In 2023, 6,069 people died by suicide in the UK, with 75% of these being men.

What about homelessness? Many people are faced with rough sleeping - living in sheds and garages, sofa surfing, or sleeping in hostels as well as on the streets. Currently more than 300,000 people are homeless on any given night in Britain. 1 in 200 households live in emergency, temporary housing.

The list goes on.

It's so easy to feel overwhelmed and helpless because of the sheer number and scale of the problems. How can we, as individuals, make a difference? Is it too overwhelming to even bother?

Once upon a time, there was an old man who used to go to the ocean to do his writing. He would walk on the beach every morning before he began his work. Early one morning, he was on the beach after a great storm had passed and found it littered with starfish as far as the eye could see, stretching in both directions.

In the distance, the old man noticed a small boy approaching. As the boy walked, he paused every so often. The man could see that he was occasionally bending down to pick up an object and throw it into the sea. The boy came closer still and the man called out, "Good morning! May I ask what you are doing?"

The young boy looked up and replied, "Throwing starfish into the ocean. The tide has washed them up onto the beach and they can't return to the sea by themselves. When the sun gets high, they will die, unless I throw them back into the water."

The old man replied, "But there must be tens of thousands of starfish on this beach. I'm afraid you won't really be able to make much of a difference."

The boy bent down, picked up another starfish and threw it as far as he could into the ocean. Then he turned, smiled, and said, "It made a difference to that one!"

We are called to make a difference to just one person whose life lies before us. To that person, we are called by Jesus to be a light bringer. Just as Jesus Christ is the Light of the World (John 8:12), so we who follow him are tasked and empowered to be lights in and to this dark world. Even if it's for just one person, we are called to spread the light of God to them so that they can see just how real Jesus is and just how deeply the Father loves them.

BRINGING HEAVEN TO EARTH

Like Josh, I believe passionately that God wants to send his Holy Spirit in a fresh outpouring on the Church, but the Church isn't to be the only beneficiary of a spiritual awakening. When God sends his Spirit to revive his Church, it is not just because he wants to see individual sinners make the journey from darkness to light. He wants to see society make that transition as well. Revival may start with individuals being profoundly impacted by the holiness, power, and love of God, but it does not end there. As someone once said, revival is not like the Dead Sea – an ocean with no outlets – but it's like the Sea of Galilee – an ocean with many rivers and tributaries. The quickest way to stop a move of God is by keeping it to ourselves. The best way to sustain it is by giving God's grace away to the lost, the lonely, and the least. What this means in practice is that newly awakened churches must not keep the light to themselves but share it. As Jesus said:

> *You're here to be light, bringing out the God-colours in the world. God is not a secret to be kept. We're going public with this, as public as a city on a hill. If I make you light bearers, you don't think I'm going to hide you under a bucket, do you? I'm putting you on a light stand. Now that I've put you there on a hilltop, on a light stand - shine!*

That's Matthew 5:15-16 in the Message paraphrase.

What I am talking about is working with our Heavenly Father to bring heaven to earth. In other words, I am talking about the Kingdom of God – God's heavenly rule made known on earth. Far too many people have historically had a very individualistic interpretation of the kingdom of heaven. They have heard the Gospel preached and repented of their sins. Putting their trust in Jesus, they have thanked God that they are now assured of going to heaven when they die. This is important. According to the Bible, everyone's a sinner and every one of us needs to confess our sins and get right with God. Revival is all about this. When God sends revival fire, his burning presence sears the consciences of sinners, causing them to recognise their unrighteousness and to look to the Cross for forgiveness. Revival history is full of glorious accounts of individuals having such encounters. As Josh will say in the next chapter, in revival seasons, people have a revelation of who God is that leads to a realisation of who they are.

But it doesn't end here. Revivals are also full of stories about how society was changed too.[1] When God pours out his Spirit, his people are envisioned and energised to take his transforming love into the darkest places, bringing his redeeming light to bear on unjust social structures – those systems that oppress rather than liberate the powerless. When this happens, Christians find themselves on a light stand. Like Florence Nightingale, they become light bearers.

This is so important. The message of the Bible is not just a **saving** Gospel – a message that brings salvation to individuals. It is also a **social** Gospel – a message of Good News to a fallen, broken society. It is especially "Good News to the poor." We cannot reduce Christianity to a religion that provides the means for individuals to go to heaven when they die. We must be far more loyal to the original founder (Jesus) and the original vision (the kingdom of God). We must inspire individual Christians to see their faith as the means by which they bring heaven to earth while they live. People in society are going through hell right now. They are poor, lonely, depressed, and oppressed, just as I wrote earlier. What we need today is to bring more of the life of heaven to those experiencing hell on earth. What revival does is release more of the power and love of the kingdom of heaven here in the world, not just in the Church. Who wouldn't want to be part of that?

FROM THE VALLEYS TO LA

The Church in the West must grasp this, not least because the younger generation - Gen Z - is driven by a passion to see justice, not just for people, but for the planet. A view of revival that is simply individualistic (i.e., about me going to heaven when I die) will not be enough to inspire this generation. Revival will need to be seen not just as something that brings salvation to individuals but something that leads to transformation outside the church. As a Forbes article has recently stated: "Millennials and Gen Zs are taking action to drive the change they want to see in the world. They are becoming more politically involved, making a conscious effort to ensure they spend their money with companies that reflect their values and pushing for change on societal issues. They believe in their individual power to make a difference, but they are also demanding that businesses and governments do their part to help build a better future."[2]

One way to increase the traction for a societal understanding of revival is by going back to the Scriptures and learning again that the mission of Jesus was not just to save sinners but to bring heaven's justice and mercy to the marginalised. This is as clear as day in the first public sermon Jesus preached in Luke 4:18.

> *"The Spirit of the Lord is on me,*
>   *because he has anointed me*
>   *to proclaim good news to the poor.*
> *He has sent me to proclaim freedom for the prisoners*
>   *and recovery of sight for the blind,*
> *to set the oppressed free,*
>   *to proclaim the year of the Lord's favour."*

The year of the Lord's favour is a reference to the Old Testament teaching about the year of Jubilee when slaves were to be freed, land restored, and debts cancelled. Sounds a bit like heaven on earth, doesn't it? At least, it does for those who are slaves, robbed of land, and poor. This was a vital part of Jesus's mission statement. He and his followers were committed not just to saving sinners; they were also committed to healing the sick and setting the captives free.

When authentic revival occurs, we see both happening. In 1904, revival broke out in the valleys of Wales. Thousands of individual souls were filled with the light of Jesus, yes, but society was changed too. The impact was so great that the police were left with nothing to do, and the courts were empty. Saloons and bars shut down for lack of business. Public drunkenness was almost non-existent. Old debts, many long forgotten, were paid off in full. Travelling theatrical agencies cancelled their engagements because everyone was in church. Profanity disappeared, and, as I wrote earlier, the pit ponies were amazed by the way they were now being treated in the mines.[3]

Two years later, revival broke out in Azusa Street, Los Angeles in what was mostly an impoverished congregation. Yet again, thousands of individuals got right with God as the Gospel was preached with great authority by people like William Seymour. But this was not the only effect of the outpouring. Sick people were healed in vast numbers – so vast, in fact, that the walls of the church building were covered in the walking sticks, hearing aids, spectacles, crutches, wheelchairs and other medical aids that had been jettisoned by those who no longer needed them. Just as dramatic, black and white skinned people now worshipped together in the same church. Racism was dealt a powerful, heavenly blow – so much so that it was said that the dividing "colour line was washed away in the blood of Christ."[4]

Sounds inspiring, doesn't it?

If you're someone whose view of revival is focused only on individuals, maybe it's time for you to remember that the Gospel is also Good News to the poor. Reclaiming the societal dimension of revival should not be a controversial or divisive matter because ministering to the powerless it is a Biblical mandate (James 1:17). The year of the Lord's favour that Jesus mentioned (i.e., the year of Jubilee) was never meant to be a literal year that began and ended sometime around 33 A.D. It's a year that's still going on and it's a timeframe that the Church needs to maximise. We are still called to bring economic and environmental justice in the name of the Lord. Anything less fails in its loyalty to a fully orbed understanding of the kingdom of heaven.

If you're someone whose view of revival is focused only on societal change, maybe it's time for you to remember that the Gospel is also Good News for sinners. The Gospel doesn't just call us to social work inspired by the mercy of Jesus. It calls us to repent of our sins, put our trust in Jesus, and to get right with a holy God.

PUT DOWN YOUR KNIVES

The founders of Methodism - John and Charles Wesley - believed that caring for the poor, prisoners, widows, and orphans was an essential part of the Christian's mission. They were concerned with remedying social injustice and worked towards the abolition of slavery. William and Catherine Booth, founders of the Salvation Army, provided homes for the homeless, agricultural training for the urban poor, and assistance for alcoholics. Dr Martin Luther King Junior - the American Baptist minister, activist, and political philosopher - led the civil rights movement, advancing his vision of justice for oppressed minorities and for racial integration in the USA. Today, in the 21st century, I am excited that what was once a rare person standing for human rights is now a large number of people motivated by their Christian faith. I can point to multiple examples of social action inspired by the Holy Spirit - foodbanks, homeless shelters, debt counselling services, youth clubs, mental-health-care projects, care for the elderly, and so on. What was once the exception is now becoming the rule.

Earlier, I wrote about the inspiring example of nurse Florence Nightingale. Interestingly, our work at ROC has recently taken us into her arena - healthcare. The National Health Service has commissioned us to run an alternative community-led mental health crisis provision in Wythenshawe, a district of Manchester. This will alleviate waiting time at the hospital accident-and-emergency department and in local doctor's surgeries. We are currently training people in mental-health first aid, working in partnership with local churches and organizations to offer a listening and signposting service to the community. I marvel that God has opened this door, and that he is raising up many Christian-led charities in the same way, such as our friends at Kintsugi Hope, Night Light Cafés, and Renew Wellbeing.[5]

We mentioned gun crime earlier. Years after we shed the name 'Gunchester', a different problem emerged. Just before Covid-19, another epidemic was sweeping the UK. The Office of National Statistics announced that 45,627 knife offences had been carried out in England and Wales in 2019. The perpetrators and victims were disproportionally young BAME (Black Asian and Minority Ethnic) men in urban areas. Of the incidents in the city of London, 61% involved people under 25 years and 25% of the victims were black.

At our ROC community engagement event commissioned by Northamptonshire Police in 2018, I interviewed a fifteen-year-old boy who said he was the only boy in his class not carrying a knife. You could feel the shock in the audience. Thames Valley Police and Crime Commissioner Matthew Barber then asked us to host a community engagement event in Reading in 2021. There had been three knife crime fatalities in Forbury Gardens in June 2020. The Bishop of Reading, the Right Reverend Olivia Graham, co-sponsored my son Josh to write the song 'Born to fly' which was filmed in Reading and performed at the ROC Conversation. It's very powerful. If you want to see and hear it, go to 'No More Knives – Josh Green, Born to Fly' on YouTube. Here are some of the lyrics:

> When it's dark and it's hard, yeah, I need you,
> Be the real you.
> You were made for more, so be the real you,
> Coz I've been there too,
> But now I gotta let this light come shine through,
> Let them see you
> You were born to fly the world needs you...
> Put down your knives,
> Coz you were born to fly.[6]

WORDS, WONDERS, AND WORKS

Justice was very much at the centre of the mission of Jesus and his followers. We should remember that the earliest church was not only characterised by the apostles' preaching (the Word) and by miracles (wonders); it was also known for its ministry to the poor (works). The Kingdom of God is therefore a three-dimensional reality; it not only comprises the **message** of Good News and the **miracles** to back that message up; it also includes acts of **mercy** directed to the poor. As Luke reports in the Book of Acts, "All the believers were together and had everything in common. They sold property and possessions to give to anyone who had need" (Acts 2:44-45). Compassionate care for those deprived of the bare necessities of life – including justice – is something we see in both Jesus's life (the Gospel of Luke) and in the lives of his followers (the Book of Acts, Luke's sequel). As early as Luke 1, Mary is declaring, "He has filled the hungry with good things but has sent the rich away empty" (v.53).

This emphasis is not just found in Luke-Acts. We should also remember Jesus's parable of the sheep and the goats in Matthew's Gospel too. On the last day of history, God will judge the world. Some will be ushered to the right side of God's throne. These are the sheep, who have done what God has asked them to do while alive on the earth. On the left, the goats will be assembled. These are a metaphor for those who failed to do what God wanted them to do on earth. The question then arises, "What does God want us to do?" If we are Christians, he wants us to bring heaven to those experiencing hell on earth. He wants us to bring the mercy and miracles of his kingdom to the hungry, thirsty, the sick, the stranger, the prisoner, and so on. This shows that God requires there to be evidence of our faith in compassionate action. Look at what the king in the story (i.e., God) says to the sheep:

'Come, you who are blessed by my Father; take your inheritance, the kingdom prepared for you since the creation of the world. For I was hungry and you gave me something to eat, I was thirsty and you gave me something to drink, I was a stranger and you invited me in, I needed clothes and you clothed me, I was sick and you looked after me, I was in prison and you came to visit me.'

Then the righteous will answer him, 'Lord, when did we see you hungry and feed you, or thirsty and give you something to drink? When did we see you a stranger and invite you in, or needing clothes and clothe you? When did we see you sick or in prison and go to visit you?'

The King will reply, 'Truly I tell you, whatever you did for one of the least of these brothers and sisters of mine, you did for me.'

(Matthew 25.34-40).

If we want to be among those blessed by our heavenly Father, we must be committed to bringing God's justice to those who are powerless and marginalised in society. I'm not saying here that we are in some way saved by good works and by acts of mercy. Rather, the Bible clearly teaches us that good works (charitable endeavours on behalf of the poor) and acts of mercy (action undertaken in a spirit of kindness and compassion) are signs that our faith is living not dead. Remember what it says in the Book of James (2:14-17). Although we are not saved *by* good works, we are saved *for* good works:

What good is it, my brothers, if someone says he has faith but does not have works? Can that faith save him? If a brother or sister has nothing to wear and has no food for the day, and one of you says to them, 'Go in peace, keep warm, and eat well,' but you do not give them the necessities of the body, what is it? So also faith of itself, if it does not have works, is dead.

INSPIRED BY THE LIGHT

Let's return to Florence Nightingale. What was the inspiration for her life of mercy and compassion? Was it some political theory or economic philosophy? No. Florence Nightingale was inspired by the Bible.[7] There were two Bible passages that became a specific source of inspiration, one in the Old Testament, the other in the New. The first was in Exodus 33:18 where Moses asked God, "Show me thy glory." God answered, "I will make all my goodness pass before thee." For Nightingale, the glory of God is his goodness. She believed that God wants us to act, to reflect God's glory to the world by making it better, through practical action. Serving as a nurse for the healing the sick was her way of doing this, showing God's goodness through compassionate work.

The second passage was Luke 1:26-38 - Mary's acceptance of her mission. This was another favourite Scripture which she quoted often, paraphrased, and widely applied. Florence Nightingale saw herself as a handmaid of the Lord and referred to other women who had taken on nursing as people called to the same role and honour. She once applied these words to herself: "Behold the handmaid of the Lord and so have I said in my youth" (Luke 1:38). To a night nurse in 1886 she said, "May we all answer the angel as Mary did: Behold the handmaid of the Lord: be it unto me according to thy word."

Florence Nightingale derived her inspiration from God's Book – the Bible – not from any human theory or philosophy. Her dream was to be a handmaiden of the Lord and, like Mary, to be unflinchingly obedient to the revelation of God's Word. That is why she wrote this in her journal on May 12th in the year 1850. "Today I am thirty - the age Christ began his mission. Now no more childish things. No more love. No more marriage. Now Lord let me think only of Thy Will, what Thou willest me to do. Oh Lord Thy Will, Thy Will."

This is what inspired her to be the Lady of the Lamp.
The Bible.
This is what will inspire us to be light bearers too.
The Word of God.
A lamp for our feet (Psalm 119:115).

SHINING CHRISTIANS

In this book, we have looked at how God is our Way Maker, Miracle Worker, Promise Keeper, and now our Light Bringer. God is glorious and resplendent beyond all imagining. In 1 Timothy 6:15-16, Paul describes him as "God, the blessed and only Ruler, the King of kings and Lord of lords, who alone is immortal and who lives in unapproachable light." That is wonderful enough. But there's more! In Christ, God has made us children of the light, so we too are light bringers, just as he is. That is why God says this in Isaiah 60:1-3:

Arise, shine, for your light has come,
and the glory of the Lord rises upon you.
See, darkness covers the earth
and thick darkness is over the peoples,
but the Lord rises upon you
and his glory appears over you.
Nations will come to your light,
and kings to the brightness of your dawn.

In his sermon, 'Shining Christians', Charles Spurgeon unpacked these verses in Isaiah 60, exhorting his congregation to increase in brightness even while the world increased in darkness.[8] To those who felt they were not very shiny, he was typically encouraging. "Little glowworm, even you must not hide your light! Sparks, tiny sparklets, you that have but one little flash, you must not conceal it, for the night is dark, and the darkness deepens."

You may be troubled by how thick the darkness is right now, but you need to understand this: this gloomy social context provides the perfect conditions in which your light can shine more brightly. The great painters have all understood this. As Leonardo da Vinci once said, "A luminous body will appear more brilliant in proportion as it is surrounded by deeper shadow." We need to be persevering and resilient. As Psalm 18:28 puts it, "You, LORD, keep my lamp burning; my God turns my darkness into light."

You may feel as if you only have a little light burning inside your heart, but a little light is better than no light at all. That little flame, even if it's as small as a pilot light, still has the capacity to dispel the darkness. As the old proverb says, "It is better to light a candle than curse the darkness." In other words, don't spend your time complaining about how bad things are. Spend your time putting the lights on wherever you're called to make a difference. A tiny flame of love has the power to remove the darkness of hate. As Dr Martin Luther King Junior once said, "Darkness cannot drive out darkness; only light can do that. Hate cannot drive out hate; only love can do that."

So, arise and shine. Be a light bearer in this dark world. Be a *shining* Christian.

I will leave the last word to Spurgeon. "Shine, for thy light shall be seen; shine, for thy light shall be useful to save life, like a lighthouse on the rock; useful to direct others home, like the cottager's candle in the window, to guide her husband to his resting-place. Shine, then, because of the good that will come of it to the world."

FOOTNOTES

1. We have mentioned Francis Asbury in this book in connection with the recent Asbury revival. Not only did Francis Asbury lead countless individuals to salvation; he also stimulated social change. See Mark Noll's article online entitled 'Spiritual Renewal and Social Transformation,' https://comment.org/spiritual-renewal-and-social-transformation/. Although in time the picture became much more complex and contentious, in these early years of US Methodism, Asbury and his followers stood against slavery as well. "We view it as contrary to the Golden Law of God on which hang all the Law and the Prophets, and the unalienable Rights of Mankind, as well as every Principle of the Revolution, to hold in the deepest Debasement, in a more abject Slavery than is perhaps to be found in any Part of the World except America, so many Souls that are capable of the Image of God."

2. For the Forbes article about Gen Z and their passion for justice, see "For Millennials and Gen Zs, Social Issues are Top of Mind." https://www.forbes.com/sites/deloitte/2021/07/22/for-millennials-and-gen-zs-social-issues-are-top-of-mind-heres-how-organizations-can-drive-meaningful-change/

3. Another aspect of social change in the Welsh revival involved the prominent and pioneering role of women in leadership. See "The Welsh Revival (1904-1905): Recovering the Role of Welsh Women", 2018 PhD thesis by Sarah Louise Prendergast:

https://radar.brookes.ac.uk/radar/items/01d79095-8ef6-47b1-819f-6dd3d0869c54/1/#:~:text=The%20Welsh%20Revival%20of%201904,be%20the%20work%20of%20God

4. See Professor Gastón Espinosa's article on divine healing at Azusa Street, Los Angeles. Espinosa is a professor of religious studies.

https://christianhistoryinstitute.org/magazine/article/power-in-the-blood-for-divine-healing

He writes: "The Apostolic Faith newspaper reported many different types of healing and miracles either at the mission itself or its daughter missions around the world. Conditions reported as healed included abscesses; addictions to alcohol, tobacco, or drugs, including opium and morphine; asthma; cancer; chills; deafness; demonic manifestations; eczema; epilepsy; eye problems, including blindness and cataracts; fever; haemorrhage; hernia; injury or malfunction of an ankle, foot, head, heart, leg, muscle, shoulder, spine, or wrist; mental illness; paralysis; pneumonia; poisoning; rheumatism; skin diseases; tuberculosis—and many others!"

5. For Renew Wellbeing see https://www.renewwellbeing.org.uk/. For Kintsugi Hope, see https://www.kintsugihope.com/. For Night Life Cafés, see https://www.actstrust.org.uk/night-light-cafes/

6. YouTube. 'NO MORE KNIVES - Josh Green Born to Fly', https://www.youtube.com/watch?v=3ERbNQHD5po

7. Lynn McDonald, PhD, "Florence Nightingale: Faith and Work", an online address at https://cwfn.uoguelph.ca/spirituality/florence-nightingale-faith-and-work/

8. Spurgeon, 'Shiny Christians,' https://www.spurgeon.org/resource-library/sermons/shining-christians/#flipbook/

CHAPTER 9

SHINING LIKE STARS (JOSH)

When it comes to God as Light Bringer, the question for us to ask is this: how brightly are we shining? In this chapter, I want to focus not just on how we are called to *bring* light but also to *be* light. We are tasked in Philippians 2:15 to "become blameless and pure", to be "children of God without fault in a warped and crooked generation." When we do this, we will shine ... "like stars in the sky." Such talk brings us to the challenging topic of holiness. We're all on journey when it comes to living a holy life. I know I am. The good news is that the God we serve walks with us on this road to becoming more like him; he is the one who strengthens and empowers us on the journey. So, this isn't about becoming modern-day Pharisees with an unhealthy striving for unattainable perfection, nor is it about creating excuses for lowering the bar of God's holy standards. It's about engaging in a healthy, balanced walk involving both personal commitment and a reliance on the Holy Spirit.

Leonard Ravenhill once said, "There's nothing worse than

a sick church in a dying world." Although that's a tough word to hear, Ravenhill was speaking the truth. Can you imagine going to a hospital in severe need of treatment only to find that all the doctors and nurses are asleep? Duncan Campbell, the evangelist who led hundreds of people to Christ in the Hebridean revival, said that many of the Christians of his day were sound in doctrine, yes, but also sound asleep. While I want to honour and respect the Church, the Bride of Christ, and while I love the local church and am very much part of one, I don't want to ignore where the Church is sick, where I'm longing for Jesus to heal us. I'm speaking to myself as someone who is part of the church, and as someone who at various times wrestles with our apathy and complacency too.

Revival history shows us that dealing with the evidence of church decline and decay - often through prayer - precedes a spiritual awakening. Some of the best examples I know showcase this great truth that it's when the darkness is darkest that God's light shines the brightest. That's why I wholeheartedly agree with my friend Andy Byrd. He's a leader in YWAM and a pioneer of a global movement called 'The Send' commissioning thousands of young people to go and make disciples. He says, "Europe is not post-Christian, it's pre-revival."[1] Amen! Revival begins with us looking in the mirror as Christians and confessing where we have chosen to walk in unrighteousness. It begins with us repenting of where we have gone wrong and resolving to get right with God.

This does not mean that we look at the Church and say that everything that's happening is useless, irrelevant, and evil. The universal Church, however sick, still carries the hope for this world. The local church, however small, is in many places alive and well, blessing communities, cities, and even countries by being on the cutting edge in serving and taking care of the poor, the elderly, the homeless, parents and toddlers, and young people in need. There is so much good in the church, both universal and local. The church is still God's primary solution for the problems of this broken world. He has not given up on his dream. The decree of the Promise Keeper still stands firm and fills us with hope: "I will build my church, and the gates of Hades will not overcome it" (Matthew 16:18). Revival does not begin with paralysing despondency. It starts with a choice to gaze at God and worship him in the beauty of who he is – our Way Maker, Miracle Worker, Promise Keeper, and Light Bringer.

WALKING IN THE LIGHT

We have already seen in this book how the human body can become sick. My mum's sudden brain bleed is an example of how this can happen, as was my father-in-law's cancer. Although our bodies were originally designed by God to be healthy, the fact that we live in a world which has fallen from the Creator's original blueprint means that we experience disease and death. The entrance of sin into the world has caused all kinds of problems, sickness being one of the most obvious and harmful. When the human body is struck down with sickness, it needs to recuperate if it is to function well again.

In the same way, the Church – which is likened to a human body by the Apostle Paul – can also become unhealthy and debilitated by the consequences of sin. 1 John 1:5-7 says this:

"This is the message we have heard from him and declare to you: God is light; in him there is no darkness at all. If we claim to have fellowship with him and yet walk in the darkness, we lie and do not live out the truth. But if we walk in the light, as he is in the light, we have fellowship with one another, and the blood of Jesus, his Son, purifies us from all sin."

Sin causes us to walk in the darkness rather than the light. John tells us we're fooling ourselves if we think otherwise. When this happens, we need to come back to walking in the light. In other words, walk with Jesus and confess our sins to him so he can heal, cleanse, and forgive us. This renews, restores, and refills us with light. It propels us afresh into the world to bring authentic light to others. When we come into the light with integrity and humility, God promises to forgive us. As 1 John 1:9 says: "If we confess our sins, he is faithful and just and will forgive us our sins and purify us from all unrighteousness."

This is something that many church leaders on the Hebrides recognised before revival broke out in 1949. In 1949, the local presbytery issued a proclamation to be read on a Sunday in all the Free Churches on the island of Lewis. It asked believers to consider the "low state of vital religion ... throughout the land ... and the present dispensation of divine displeasure ... due to growing carelessness toward public worship ... and the growing influence of the spirit of pleasure which has taken growing hold of the younger generation." The proclamation called on the churches to "take these matters to heart and to make serious inquiry what must be the end if there be no repentance." Many people in the Hebrides took this matter to heart themselves. They didn't engage in finger pointing but instead set about getting right with God themselves. This is what we need in our prayers – heartfelt transparency before God – the kind of thing that Jesus called for in the comparison between the Pharisee and the tax collector (Luke 18:9-14).

"Then Jesus told this story to some who had great confidence in their own righteousness and scorned everyone else: Two men went to the Temple to pray. One was a Pharisee, and the other was a despised tax collector. The Pharisee stood by himself and prayed this prayer: 'I thank you, God, that I am not like other people—cheaters, sinners, adulterers. I'm certainly not like that tax collector! I fast twice a week, and I give you a tenth of my income.'

But the tax collector stood at a distance and dared not even lift his eyes to heaven as he prayed. Instead, he beat his chest in sorrow, saying, 'O God, be merciful to me, for I am a sinner.'

I tell you, this sinner, not the Pharisee, returned home justified before God. For those who exalt themselves will be humbled, and those who humble themselves will be exalted."

Here Jesus highlights the prayer of authentic humility. As Psalm 51:17 says, "The sacrifice you desire is a broken spirit. You will not reject a broken and repentant heart, O God." This is what the tax collector demonstrates. While the Pharisee is looking down on the tax collector with condescension, the tax collector is looking up to Jesus with desperation. My prayer is that all of us, me included, would pray like the tax collector, sharing our hearts with God humbly and honestly. Only this way will we be full of light.

MAINTAINING HEALTHY EYES

In case you think I'm being a bit intense here, remember what Jesus taught about our eyes being like lamps in our bodies:

"No one lights a lamp and puts it in a place where it will be hidden, or under a bowl. Instead, they put it on its stand, so that those who come in may see the light. Your eye is the lamp of your body. When your eyes are healthy, your whole body also is full of light. But when they are unhealthy, your body also is full of darkness. See to it, then, that the light within you is not darkness. Therefore, if your whole body is full of light, and no part of it dark, it will be just as full of light as when a lamp shines its light on you" (Luke 11:33-36).

The logic of what Jesus teaches here is crystal clear. He warns us that if we are careful about what we look at, and if we choose to look only at what is pure and healthy, then our bodies will be filled with light. This will empower us to be light bringers. If, on the other hand, we are careless with our eyes, and if we choose to look at what is impure and unhealthy, then our bodies will be filled with darkness. This will disempower us from being light bringers.

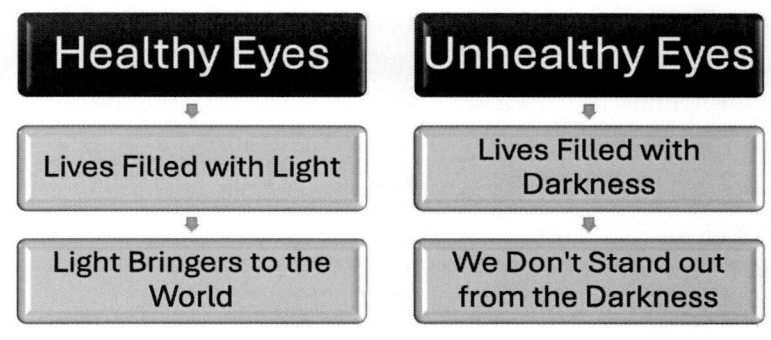

I mainly wear contact lenses as my eyesight without them is quite poor. This means I regularly go to the opticians for checkups. Opticians help us to determine how clear our vision is. If our eyesight has become impaired, we have glasses or lenses made for us. Sometimes we need upgrades if our sight has regressed. This same sort of care needs to be embraced when it comes to the spiritual and moral side of our lives. We need to take time to ensure that our spiritual eyes are healthy too. The Greek word for unhealthy in Luke 11:33-36 is *poneros* which means evil or diseased. It's a word with a serious connotation – one that reminds me of 2 Chronicles 7:14 where God calls us to turn from our *wicked ways* if we are to experience him healing our land.

As Jesus trained his disciples, he cautioned them against allowing their eyes to become unhealthy. This is even more relevant today than it was two thousand years ago. Today, we have become a highly visual culture. We spend inordinate amounts of time with our eyes glued to the small screens of our smartphones and tablets, consuming huge quantities of information at a speed that people one hundred years ago would have found unimaginable. This includes data that can be used for healthy or unhealthy purposes, depending on the influencer communicating to them and the observers consuming them. Some of what's transmitted to our eyes through these screens is unquestionably unhealthy. It fills our minds and bodies with darkness. How can we be light bringers in the public online space if we are not ensuring that our eyes are healthy in our private lives? Our eyes are not just like lamps. They are portals. We need to guard the optical gates of our bodies, and we need to do so with vigilance.

ATTENDING TO OUR EARS

In 2020, the Lord called me to a fresh consecration of my ears. This was something specific and personal to my situation at the time. I was involved with the music industry and making songs on a regular basis. During that time, I found myself absorbing all sorts of music. My 'ear gate' was unguarded. Early in 2021, I sensed the Lord calling me to listen only to music about Jesus, to consecrate my 'ear gate', and to glorify him with what I heard. This was important to me because years before I had heard someone prophesy with extraordinary accuracy. This caused me to wonder how someone could hear the Lord speak so clearly. I sensed God saying, "You could hear me more clearly if your ears weren't so dirty." Ouch! During the Covid lockdown, the Lord reminded me of this at a time when he was drawing me deeper into his Word and into prayer. God asked me to reconsecrate my ears.

It only took a few days of listening only to music about

Jesus and already I was hearing God more clearly. I was having regular encounters with him and experiencing a deep sense of peace and joy. What I thought would be a burden quickly became a blessing. What started out as a discipline soon became a delight. After some time of doing this, I spoke at a youth gathering and the Holy Spirit moved in miraculous ways as many young people poured forward to dedicate their whole lives to Jesus. That night, I heard God speak so clearly as I prophesied over the young people that I almost surprised myself. They told me afterwards it spoke exactly to their lives. One youth leader called to tell me they had baptised eight of their young people in the wake of it all. Of course, this is all a work of God's Spirit, but we know that he is looking for open and empty vessels through which to work.

Consecration in the private place led to a fresh demonstration of God's power in the public space. Choosing to be filled with the light in my own life led to being a light bringer to others.

It's time to consecrate our eyes and ears!

THE PRIVATE AND THE PUBLIC

Who we are behind the scenes, and what we focus on when no one else is looking, determines the power and authority we walk in when operating in the public space. When we give ourselves to prayer in private, God releases his power through us in public. But this isn't just about prayer, although it certainly helps us get there; it's about holiness and integrity. God is watching us all the time. What he sees in us when no one is looking is a vital factor in what he does through us when everyone is watching. What flows out of us when we are with others is a sign of what we've allowed to fill our lives when we are on our own.

In Acts 19:11-16 we find an interesting passage about a group of people who were trying to operate in the power of God's Spirit in public without truly knowing God in private:

Some Jews who went around driving out evil spirits tried to invoke the name of the Lord Jesus over those who were demon-possessed. They would say, "In the name of the Jesus whom Paul preaches, I command you to come out." Seven sons of Sceva, a Jewish chief priest, were doing this. One day the evil spirit answered them, "Jesus I know, and Paul I know about, but who are you?" Then the man who had the evil spirit jumped on them and overpowered them all. He gave them such a beating that they ran out of the house naked and bleeding."

James Aladiran says, "I can deceive you, and you can deceive me, but there is no fooling the spirit-realm."[2] We can see that here. The demons knew who the seven sons of Sceva really were. These men didn't know Jesus, they just wanted to operate in his power the same way Paul did. In the verses just before this passage, Luke tells us that "God did extraordinary miracles through Paul, so that even handkerchiefs and aprons that had touched him were taken to the sick, and their illnesses were cured and the evil spirits left them." Paul knew Jesus in the private place, so he could operate in spiritual authority in the public place. This is the exact opposite of the sons of Sceva.

I'm not saying here that miracles are a sign of God's approval of us. In Matthew 7, Jesus told people who did many wonders in his name that he didn't even know them. Miracles are not a reliable indicator when it comes to people's spiritual state. Jesus is simply reminding us that if we want to operate in spiritual authority, if we want to bring light to a dark world, we need to know the one who is light.

I live in Manchester, so I can tell you the name of Manchester United's stadium and their players. I can even tell you their league position right now, but all this is head knowledge because I don't follow that team as a fan. With head knowledge, I can easily fool someone who doesn't know that I'm not a United supporter into thinking that I am one. But I'm actually a Manchester City supporter! I am a fan of their arch-rivals. I know about Manchester United in my head. I support Manchester City in my heart.

The sons of Sceva knew about Jesus in their heads, but not in their hearts. Their lack of private devotion portrayed the true state of their hearts, and they ultimately received the full consequences for their insincerity. Jesus warns us that knowing him in a personal, consecrated way is what matters most in the end.

"Not everyone who says to me, 'Lord, Lord,' will enter the kingdom of heaven, but only the one who does the will of my Father who is in heaven. Many will say to me on that day, 'Lord, Lord, did we not prophesy in your name and in your name drive out demons and, in your name, perform many miracles?' Then I will tell them plainly, 'I never knew you. Away from me, you evildoers!'" (Matthew 7:21-23).

Jesus is much more interested in our private intimacy than our public activity. It may not feel like it, but this is actually very good news! Why? Because Jesus wants to know us. He's not looking for burned-out, stressed-out servants; he's after faithful and loving friends. He wants us to prioritise his presence in private over our performance in public. As churches in the West, we've spent a lot of money, time, and effort on public performance. What about God's presence? Have we made this our priority? Have we put as much investment in ministering *to* him as we have in ministering *for* him?

I believe we need to become hungrier for the holy presence of God if we are to see revival in our day. Me included. If we get that right, everything else will fall into place. Jesus says, "Seek first his kingdom and his righteousness, and all these things will be given to you as well" (Matthew 6:33). The apostles followed this order of priorities. In Acts 1, Jesus told them to wait for the Holy Spirit. They obeyed him and kept praying until the fire fell from heaven on the Day of Pentecost. For them, waiting for the manifest presence of God was more important than anything else. They could have prioritised activities associated with being a church – such as preaching the Gospel and feeding the hungry - but they prioritised praying for the promised gift of the Spirit. Once God poured out his Spirit, everything else – such as signs, wonders, and miracles – was given to them as well. Consequently, they didn't chase miracles; miracles chased them.

SHINING LIKE STARS (JOSH)

HEAVENLY PRIORITIES

In Isaiah chapter 6, the prophet describes a vision of some angelic creatures before the throne of God. Their sole purpose is to gaze upon the beauty of the Lord and to bathe in the fiery glow of God's presence. In Isaiah 6:2-3, he says,

> *"Above him were seraphim, each with six wings: With two wings they covered their faces, with two they covered their feet, and with two they were flying. And they were calling to one another:*
> *'Holy, holy, holy is the Lord Almighty; the whole earth is full of his glory'."*

What's interesting about these creatures is that four out of their six wings were used to cover themselves. The other two wings they used to fly. Wings are normally designed for flight, but two thirds of the wings on these seraphim were used to express faceless adoration. What if we, in our lives as Jesus's followers, were to reflect these priorities? How this works practically is different for each of us, but the call for our hearts to be wholly devoted to Jesus remains. It's intimacy before activity. What if we made our main priority as a people of God, well, God? Jesus wants the Father's house, the church, to be a place of adoration more than he wants it to be a place of activity, especially consumeristic activity. Isn't this why Jesus castigated his contemporaries in the Temple? Jesus said, "It is written, 'My house will be called a house of prayer,' but you are making it 'a den of robbers'." (Matthew 21:13).

This is how we are healed as a sick church, when we start prioritising what Jesus wants us to prioritise. When we go out into the world having spent time in the presence of God, we will find that what we say and do has much greater power than if we go straight out onto the streets in our own strength.

When we pray, we spend time with a God who died on the Cross to save the world. When we pray, we're filled with his heart for a lost and dying world and we're sent out to make a difference, with the power of the Spirit igniting and inspiring us. That's why, after Isaiah's heavenly vision of the seraphim, he cried, "Here I am, send me." Spending time in the light was what compelled him to be a light bringer to the world. Prayer fuelled his desire to spread the light. Remember, 'seraphim' means 'burning ones.' Even the name of these creatures is a clue!

HOLINESS VERSUS PERFECTION

Remember the subject of the song sung by the seraphim - "Holy, Holy, Holy." When the Bible wants to emphasise a point, it uses repetition. We can conclude from the repeated use of "holy" that the holiness of God is of paramount importance. This is what the burning ones celebrate as they spend time close to God.

Holiness speaks of the moral perfection and purity of God. It also denotes his separateness from all other beings – his absolute uniqueness. What if this is what the world saw in the Church? Of course, we'll never fully match God himself, but he did command, "Be holy as I am holy." Are we seeking to be so full of the light of God's holiness that we dispel the darkness wherever we place our feet? Do we make holiness a priority, as the seraphim did? This has always been a priority in revival. Before the fire of revival has fallen, people – even small numbers of people – have come to a crushing awareness of their lack of holiness and have sought to get right with God. It will be no different in our time.

Only those who are prepared to be refined in the fire can be carriers of the fire. When we submit to this process, we can become light bringers because we're walking in the light. This is one of the big lessons of revival history. The men and women God has used most powerfully during historic outpourings have always gone through a process of repentance first. They have consecrated their entire lives to God, letting God remove every trace of darkness. Once that happened, they were fit to become God's light bringers.

Please note this very important point, however. This isn't about striving for *perfection* like modern-day Pharisees. It's about being led by the Spirit into *holiness*.

Perfection is the fruit of legalism – of striving to be righteous in our own strength. Holiness, on the other hand, is the product of grace – of being empowered by the Spirit. Perfection is about self-righteous, performance-based piety. Holiness is about pursuing Christ's righteousness out of love. I'm not saying holiness doesn't require our participation; we must partner with God to see this come to pass in our lives. We need to open up to God, receive his power, and allow his Spirit to rule and reign in our lives.

Isaiah's consecration started with a dramatic revelation and proceeded to a profound realisation. He had a revelation of who God is – the one who is holy - and this led to a realisation of what he was – a man with unclean lips. This realisation produced repentance, and this repentance produced the restoration of his calling and purpose. None of us is perfect, nor will we ever truly be until we're perfected in heaven, but we can all pursue a holy God so that his holiness permeates our being. We need to encounter God and continually encounter him. To do that we must consistently make ourselves ready and available to him as we minister in his presence.

BEHOLDING AND BECOMING

There's an old saying – you become like what you behold. If the seraphim teach us anything in Isaiah 6 it's that where we choose to focus our attention is vital for our spiritual and moral transformation. This is called the law of unconscious assimilation. This states that we become like the people we most admire, the people in whose presence we spend the most amount of time.

One time, I was praying, and I asked God what was on his heart. We often tell God what is on our hearts and give him a list of issues and needs. This isn't a wrong thing to do, by the way; Jesus taught us to pray about our needs when he said, "Give us this day our daily bread." But he also taught us to pray, "Let *your* Kingdom come, let *your* will be done, on earth as it is in heaven." I therefore want my prayers to be concerned with God's desires not just my own.

After I prayed, I sensed God saying, "Not many people look

at my creation anymore." I was quite surprised by this, but it made me realise that we are so consumed with screens we miss the wonder and beauty of the world around us. We are captivated by devices that are making us captives. Those who have conducted research into the effects of this trend tell us that this obsession with small screen devices is making us more anxious and stressed. Yet, we also know that God's creation, as we walk in it and behold it, is highly beneficial for our mental health. Remember what Psalm 121:1 says: "I look to the hills, where does my help come from, my help comes from the Lord, the maker of heaven and earth".

Today, we are more preoccupied with consuming trivia that amuses us than we are contemplating what awakens our wonder. This is true for our relationship with the magnificence of God's love which, as the Welsh revival hymn-writer put it, is "as vast as the ocean." Of course, we can use small-screen technology to reach people for Jesus, and so we should, but the call to holiness is crucial because this is our USP – our unique selling point. People will start coming to Jesus when they see a generation once held captive by screens now captivated by God. Here's a good prayer if you agree. "Turn away my eyes from looking at worthless things and revive me in your way" (Psalm 119:37).

THREE SPIRITUAL PRIORITIES

I'm reminded of a saying often attributed to St Francis: "Go throughout the world and preach the Gospel. If necessary, use words." We do need to use words to preach the Gospel, but the challenge is for our lives to preach too, sometimes even more than our words. As the old saying goes, "there are three testaments that other people read: the Old Testament, the New Testament, and the *You* Testament. The You Testament is the one that most non-Christians read first."

At some point, maybe after seeing our reactions to difficult situations, someone should be asking us, "So, why do you live this way?" "Why weren't you angry?" "Why did you forgive that person?" Seeing how we live should stimulate and provoke people to ask why we behave the way we do. What they *see* in us should cause them to want to *hear* from us. Their curious *eyes* should give them attentive *ears*. Then when we speak the name of Jesus it will be backed up by having seen Jesus at work in our lives. The combination of the Gospel proclaimed in Word and deed has incredible power.

If we are to become more luminous in the world, we must prioritise private consecration leading to public demonstration. This is especially important for Gen Z - those born between 1997 and 2012 (aged 12 to 27 years old as of 2024). That's why I've recently launched a brand-new ministry called *Gen Zeal*, born from a longing to see the next generation lead revival through holy passion, fervent prayer, and bold proclamation. I believe God is raising not "Gen Z", with all its negative stereotypes, but "Gen Zeal" - a generation on fire for God that will usher in a great move of God and reverse the statistics of decline in the Western church.

What will this look like?

Part of this move of God will be characterised by what we call 'consecrated creativity' - young people using their gifts and talents to express the message of following Jesus wholeheartedly. Through social media, music and the arts, prayer meetings, mentoring, preaching, equipping and training events, and above all through encountering God we're believing for the next generation to lead the way. We're calling and contending for a shift to take place in the world of young people and young adults that will bring revival. Through being light, we're believing that an army of young people will bring light to a dark world.

The Lord invites all of us, no matter our age, into this call. I believe there are three practical priorities and spiritual postures that God wants us to embrace.

1. Being Deeply Rooted in the Word

Isaiah 8:20 says, "If they do not speak according to this word, it is because there is no light in them." God's Word is a light for our feet. If we don't spend time in God's Word, we will lose our way. As Psalm 119:9 asks, "How can a young person stay on the path of purity? By living according to your Word." Living according to God's Word is how we walk in the light and therefore bring light to others. This is more than just a matter of reading the Bible from time to time; it's a call to plant deep roots in the soil of the Scriptures. That way, just as Jesus used God's Word to resist the devil in the wilderness, we will be able to displace the darkness in the world by the light of God's truth.

2. Being Dedicated to Private Prayer

We should never underestimate the effectiveness of our prayer lives. Every time we spend time in the secret place with our heavenly Father, we grow shinier for him. Remember what God told Moses to say to Aaron in Numbers 6:22-26:

> *"The Lord bless you*
> *and keep you;*
> *the Lord make his face shine on you*
> *and be gracious to you;*
> *the Lord turn his face toward you*
> *and give you peace."*

When we spend time in the presence of God in private, we enjoy the brightness of our Father's smiling face. This was something Moses knew from his own personal experience. As we read in Exodus 34, when Moses had solitary face-to-face encounters with God, the skin of his face would become radiant.

3. Being a Devoted Disciple of Jesus

I have recently been struck by the simple words of an old and familiar song about deciding to follow Jesus, no turning back. This song has long been sung in church meetings across the world, but not many people know its origins. The words were first spoken by a man called Nokseng in north-east India in the late 19th century. As a village chief threatened Nokseng and his wife and children, Nokseng – a local man - said: "I have decided to follow Jesus. Though no one joins me, still I will follow. The cross before me, the world behind me. No turning back."[3] No sooner had he finished saying this than they were all martyred for their faith. Not long afterwards, the entire village community, including the chief who ordered the execution, decided to follow Jesus.

Matthew 24:14 says, "And this gospel of the kingdom will be preached in the whole world as a testimony to all nations, and then the end will come." As I wrote earlier in this book, the word 'testimony' is the word in Greek from which we get 'martyr'. To be a testimony to the world of who Jesus is, we need to be fully sold out, with lives laid down, all-in for Jesus. If the Gospel is to be preached to the whole world – something possible today because of the global connectivity provided by the worldwide web – we must be devoted disciples of Jesus. The closer we follow the one who is the Light of the World, the more we will become light bringers. More and more will then come to declare the truth of Isaiah 9:2. "The people walking in darkness have seen a great light; on those living in the land of deep darkness a light has dawned."

FOOTNOTES

1. Andy Byrd says this here https://www.instagram.com/andybyrd1/reel/Cn2bh03PQV-/?hl=en

2. James Aladiran shares about this here https://www.youtube.com/watch?v=KsTlx1Rm_S0

3. https://youth.opendoorsuk.org/i-have-decided-to-follow-jesus/

CHAPTER 10

AS HE IS, SO ARE WE (DEBRA/JOSH)

It wouldn't be right to end this book without turning for a moment from who God is to what we are called to be as his children here in the world. As we have seen, God is our Way Maker, Miracle Worker, Promise Keeper, and Light Bringer. He is many more things besides, of course. No one can ever say all there is to say about the goodness and glory of God. If we could sum him up, he would cease to be God. God is beyond human description. Finite words will never fully capture his infinite nature. That said, God is these four things, and we celebrate these multifaceted aspects of his nature. In this book, we have turned the diamond of his character in the light of his Word and reflected the colourful radiance of each of these four facets, sharing our own experience of these refracted truths by pointing to how we have seen them especially in adversity.

This emphasis on what we have both experienced leads us not only to talk about how we have been blessed but how we are to bless other people. Remember, God has created us in his image. As we read in Genesis 1:26-27: "God said, 'Let us make man in our image, according to our likeness, and let them rule over the fish of the sea and over the birds of the sky and over the cattle and over all the earth.' And God created man in his own image, in the image of God he created him; male and female he created them." We are not just called to receive the blessings we have been talking about in this book. We are also called to pass them on to others. As someone once said, the paradox of God's blessing is this: you can't keep it unless you give it away.

In Christ, God came to dwell among us in a human body. He wants to do the same thing with us. We are the Body of Christ on earth. Mother Teresa came to understand what this implied. She famously said, "I used to pray that God would feed the hungry, or do this or that, but now I pray that he will guide me to do whatever I'm supposed to do, what I can do. I used to pray for answers, but now I'm praying for strength. I used to believe that prayer changes things, but now I know that prayer changes us, and we change things."[1] So, while God is the ultimate version of the aspects of his character we have looked at, nonetheless, we too can help people we can help people find a way where there is no way; we can pray for them to receive miracles; we can share the promises of God with them; we can be light bringers in the darkness that surrounds them. We can be an answer.

As we wrote earlier, Jean Darnell prophesied that God will one day use anointed communicators in the UK and these people will carry the fire of God's presence to the world. In this book, we have interpreted this as a move of God using the world wide web. What if the greatest influencers in the future were people sold out for Jesus? What if the creators that people most wanted to watch and hear were those who show ordinary people all over the world how they can find a way where there seems to be no way, how they can receive an intervention from heaven, how they can find a hope and a future in the promises of God, how they can have the darkness in their lives replaced by the light? What if those who have been powerfully blessed by these multifaceted ways of God were to devote themselves with excellence and eloquence to blessing others with the unique wisdom they have acquired? People today are desperate for lasting and life-changing wisdom. What if you are the ones, like Joseph and Daniel, to carry and communicate it?

But God doesn't just want us to be a *virtual* presence. He wants us to live among other people, to serve them, to show them his ways, to pray for them to receive a miracle, to share his promises with them face-to-face, to be a shining light as we walk and talk with them in person. Virtual communication is important. Physical communication – being Christ's presence to other people – is crucial. Paul speaks of pouring himself out like a drink offering for the service of others and for the sake of the Gospel (Philippians 2:17; 2 Timothy 4:6). In other words, we're blessed to be a blessing. We are not simply called to pray for others, as powerful and profound as that is; we're also meant to do something about their needs. We're meant to show them a way out of their troubles, to pray for them to receive a divine breakthrough, to share the promises of God, to radiate God's light.

Who in your network is in need today? What do you have in your hand that you can pass on to them? We are like the boy with the loaves and fishes, or Moses with his staff. God hasn't left us empty-handed as we seek to help others. He multiplies and anoints what little we have. However ordinary and mundane these things may seem, with God's help they can become agents of change. By giving away what we have, even if it seems like we don't have much to offer, it's amazing how God can use our little and do a lot with it. As Ephesians 3:20 tells us, God "is able to do immeasurably more than all we ask or imagine, according to his power that is at work within us."

Josh writes, "I recently did a study on how many times the Bible records God acting independently of mankind, and then a study of when he works in cooperation with human beings. I found only a small number of examples when the former happened – like creation, the plagues in Egypt, and the resurrection of Jesus. But even then, what's interesting is the fact that in every instance when God acts independently from us, he still involves humans. At creation, he made human beings. At the end of the plagues, he sought to set his people free. At the resurrection of Jesus, he provided the way for human beings to be saved. This shows, even when God wills or works something independently from us, his heart is always towards us.

According to my research, in the Bible God seems to act this way 10% of the time. The other 90%, God works through us. He invites us into his story. So, Moses leads God's people out of slavery. David fights God's battles. Joshua takes the people into the Promised Land. The prophets speak to God's people. John prepares the way. Mary gives birth to Jesus. 120 disciples of Jesus pray for the Holy Spirit, and the first Christians evangelise much of the Roman Empire in just over two decades. It reminds me of what Amos 3:7 says: 'Surely the Sovereign LORD does nothing without revealing his plan to his servants the prophets'." God wants us to be part of his plans!

Where does all this leave us?

In the words of Pastor Karen Wheaton, "you matter!"

You're here on purpose, for a purpose.

Your life is important to God.

He wants to work with and through you.

Jesus Christ is our Way Maker, Miracle Worker, Promise Keeper, and Light Bringer. The Bible tells us this. But the Bible also says, "as he is, so are we in this world" (1 John 4:17, NKJV). As Jesus Christ is in heaven, so are we on earth. This even applies to the call to do miracles. We too can pray for these. In fact, Jesus said, "Very truly I tell you, whoever believes in me will do the works I have been doing, and they will do *even greater things* than these, because I am going to the Father." (John 14:12). Greater means "greater in number." While Jesus was ministering two thousand years ago, he could only do miracles in one place at a time. Now, thanks to the outpouring of the Holy Spirit, we can pray for miracles everywhere. As Jesus promised, "And these signs will follow those who believe: In my name they will cast out demons; they will speak with new tongues; they will take up serpents; and if they drink anything deadly, it will by no means hurt them; they will lay hands on the sick, and they will recover" (Mark 16:17-18).

We are called to live in the truth of 1 John 4:17: As Christ is (in heaven), so are we in this world. What if we took this seriously? There would be revival. Remember, God has promised to send his Spirit. In Joel 2, he promised to send a mighty revival in "the last days." This means there's more to come than we've ever dreamed! If God did it through the people who've gone before us - ordinary men and women like you and me - then what's to stop him doing it through us? God's power is made perfect in our weakness. If you feel you don't qualify, that's the very thing that qualifies you.

In all this, we need to remember that it's not by human strength but by God's Spirit that we do what God requires of us (Zechariah 4:6). This is a call that we cannot possibly fulfil while relying only on our own resources. We must hold on to hope and cling to Jesus as he walks with us through the valleys. We need to have faith if we are to continue to believe that miracles can happen. We need strength to persevere until God's promises come to pass. We need God's resources if, like John the Baptist, we are to burn like lamps in the darkness. The good news is we don't do all this in our own strength alone. We have a God who works unceasingly on our behalf. He does not grow weary. His arm is not too short to save. His power is made perfect in our weakness. He fights our battles. He never leaves nor forsakes us. All we need to do is call on him, and he will come to our aid.

So, as this book concludes, let's pray together.

Everlasting Father, Prince of peace, we come to you, the author and perfector of our faith. Some of us come broken, hurting, and wounded by all this life throws at us. Others of us come fired up, ready to take on the world.

You alone have the power to save, heal, redeem, and restore.

AS HE IS, SO ARE WE (DEBRA/JOSH)

We ask that you make that power available to us as we bring ourselves, our loved ones, our communities, and this fractured world before you. Let your presence surround and fill us so that we can become more aware of how you make a way where there is no way, how you do miracles, how you fulfil your promises, how you bring light to this dark world. Then, show us how we can faithfully reflect your image in us by sharing these same blessings with others.

Let your Holy Spirit work through us as we pray and believe for the greater things you've promised.

Fill us with fresh faith and strength.

And send revival, Lord.

Please send revival.

In Jesus's name.

Amen.

FOOTNOTES

1. https://blogs.glowscotland.org.uk/ed/turnbullvva/quotes-from-mother-teresa/

ENDORSEMENTS

Way Maker is a powerful testament to the faithfulness of God in the darkest seasons of life. Through deeply personal and heartfelt storytelling, Debra and Josh take readers on a journey of hope, showing that God is not only a Miracle Worker but also a Promise Keeper and Light Bringer. Whether you are a parent praying for your child, a leader facing unseen struggles, or someone seeking reassurance in life's valleys, this book will encourage you to trust in God's many ways of working. A must read for anyone longing to see God's hand in both the sudden and the gradual.

Marie Aitken, Senior Relationship Manager, Alpha UK

The Lord often allows his prophetic voices to become a message before they get to preach or teach it. In *Way Maker*, Debra and Josh Green teach profound lessons on the power of prayer and the various ways in which God works in our lives, especially in challenging times. There's an authority that they both carry to bring this message to the body of Christ because they have lived and are living it. This book will be an encouragement to anyone needing a boost in their walk of faith.

James Aladiran, Founder, Prayer Storm

The beauty of this book is in its mother-and-son combination. Debra and Josh share their experiences of life with honesty and openness. This evidently strong relationship enriches the content and points to a loving heavenly Father who can be trusted through every season of life. It will particularly speak to those on a quest to know more of God's presence.

Stuart Bell, Founding leader of Ground Level Network and Alive Church

Way Maker is a heartfelt and encouraging read for anyone seeking to deepen their understanding of faith in the face of life's challenges. Debra and Josh Green's emphasis on prayer, presence, and the multifaceted ways in which God operates in our lives invites readers to find hope and comfort in their darkest moments. This book serves as a reminder that, regardless of the situation, God is always present, walking alongside us as we navigate the complexities of life.

Dan Blythe, Global Youth Director, Alpha International

For over twenty years, I've seen first-hand how Debra, her husband Frank, and the family have navigated life and faith. They can speak into both mountain-top experiences as well as those in the dark valleys of life. This profound book challenges the common expectation that God's intervention should always be sudden and miraculous. Instead, it reassures every believer that God is a Way Maker who often leads us *through* trials rather than simply removing them. The authors also emphasize that persistent prayer is crucial, even when it *seems* ineffective. He is always at work, and no prayer is wasted - even when the outcome is different from our expectations. I am so grateful this book has been given life.

Tania Bright, Co-Chief Executive Officer, Home for Good

What an incredible book! Raw, powerful, and inspiring! *Way Maker* is packed with authentic stories that not only kept me at the edge of my seat, but most of all made me in awe of a Way-Maker God who intervenes and walks with us through fire. It brought me to my knees to pray, and it made me even hungrier for revival in our generation. Read on and let your soul be stirred and faith be built!

Sarah Breuel, Executive Director of Revive Europe

Way Maker is a passionate and heartfelt invitation to know the Lord more fully, journey through our storms with him, dream bigger dreams for our places and relationships, and start living the lives for which we were made. Honest, practical, biblical, and inspiring, this book is such a gift to the Church in this hour.

Gavin Calver, CEO, Evangelical Alliance

What a precious thing that Debra and Josh Green would come together to write such an encouraging and faith-building book. I've journeyed with them both for decades now and been privileged to witness many of these Jesus-only stories up close and personally. Read on and be inspired!

Andy Hawthorne, Global CEO, The Message Trust

Way Maker is not just an exciting chronicle of how God has opened ways in the past but an encouraging challenge to pray for him to open even greater ways in the future.

Canon J. John, Evangelist, Philo Trust

Way Maker is an honest and inspiring read by mother-and-son team, Debra and Josh Green. I've known "the Greens" for more than two decades. It is so moving to read about journeys, as individuals and as a family, in which faith and enduring hope shine through so strongly.

Billy Kennedy, International Leader Pioneer Network

Nothing beats seeing different generations working together for the expansion of God's kingdom on earth. This collaboration by Debra and Josh Green chronicles their journey of faith and the importance of having a deep understanding and relationship with God to live a life of purpose. It is a must read for anyone desiring a deeper relationship with God. It comes highly recommended.

Pastor Abimbola Komolafe, Senior Pastor Jubilee Church Manchester RCCG

There is something so significant about a parent and child's journey. Debra and Josh have an amazing adventure together of God's grace, faithfulness, goodness, and breakthrough power. I encourage you to allow this book to raise faith, challenge misconceptions, and encourage your spirit.

Dan Randall – NXT Move Europe, The Way UK, and Life Church, Lancashire

ENDORSEMENTS

Debra and Josh have given us a monumental invitation to join the story of God - the story of the ultimate Way Maker. From Israel's journey to freedom to Jesus coming to earth, Scripture testifies to God's supernatural intervention. Through their own remarkable stories, Debra and Josh reveal how the Way Maker is still at work today. For those in need of something only a Way-Making, Miracle-Working, Promise-Keeping, Light-Bringing God can give, this book is a bold call to join him in transforming your family and friends, your community, and our lost and hurting world. My faith for a move of God has grown page by page!

Joe Reeser, Senior Pastor Ramp Church Manchester

I have absolutely loved reading *Way Maker*. We can get so stuck looking at our feet that we forget to look up and see the majesty of God. This book takes us through some of the descriptive names of God to help us say "Wow!" I would champion this book for new Christians wanting to understand the power, majesty, and miracles of God, while also encouraging more established followers to reconnect with the supernatural move of God. Why not take the time to remind yourself of the way that God makes for your life, the miracles in store, and the promises he has already made, so we can be the light in the darkness?

Rev Dr Cris Rogers, All Hallows Bow

For additional resources, visit our website:
www.roc.uk.com/waymaker

BIOS

JOSH GREEN

After a decade working at The Message Trust as an evangelist, Josh and a group of friends went on to set up an international organisation, recorded and wrote music that has been streamed millions of times, and preached the Gospel to thousands of young people globally. He gained a BA in Kingdom Theology at Westminster Theological Centre while acting as their Programme Director for the Church Planting and Leadership course. He also worked with Prayerstorm.

Josh and his wife Emma helped plant and lead a church in Manchester (UK) for five years before joining the Ramp Church which they now attend and where they serve with their three children - Liberty, Simeon, and Halle-Rose.

Josh pioneered exciting youth initiatives for several years as the national youth director for 24-7 Prayer and Wildfires Youth. He has now stepped into a new faith-filled journey of leading a brand-new international organisation called Gen Zeal.

Josh loves great coffee, deep conversation, being with his family, a good curry, and Manchester City. He is an author, content creator, passionate leader, bold communicator, and someone committed to raising the next generation, serving the local church, and being more like Jesus every day.

Website - www.genzeal.net
Instagram - @joshgreen1.0
Instagram - @genzeal_
Email - team@genzeal.net

BIOS

DEBRA GREEN (OBE)

Debra Green is the national director and founder of Redeeming Our Communities (ROC), a registered charity founded in 2004. For thirty years, she has been bringing organisations together to work towards the goal of social transformation, starting with her home city of Manchester. Since 2004, this work has expanded, and she has acted as a consultant to many other towns and cities with significant results. This has attracted interest from public services and local authorities. In 2012, she received an OBE in recognition of services to community cohesion and was recently appointed a Deputy Lieutenant in Greater Manchester.

Debra is married to Frank. They have four grownup children and seven grandchildren.

Frank and Debra led a church together in South Manchester. She is frequently asked to speak at events and conferences.

Debra is the co-author (with Frank) of *City-Changing Prayer* (2005), and author of *ROC Your World – Changing Communities for Good* (2014), and *Mountain Moving Prayer* (2019). She authored the *Serve Workbook* for Spring Harvest

(2022). Her books and resources are on sale in the ROC website shop (www.roc.uk.com).

email info@roc.uk.com
X @debrajgreen
Instagram @debrajeangreen
X @weareroc
Insta @wearerocuk
LinkedIn www.linkedin.com/in/debragreenobe